Strands of Memory
—*My Swan Song*

Sweet and Bittersweet Memories
and Meditations

William R. Tracey, Ed.D.

Order this book online at www.trafford.com
or email orders@trafford.com

Most Trafford titles are also available at major online book retailers.

Printed in the United States of America.

ISBN: 978-1-4669-4463-3 (sc)
ISBN: 978-1-4669-4462-6 (e)

Trafford rev. 09/06/2012

 www.trafford.com

North America & international
toll-free: 1 888 232 4444 (USA & Canada)
phone: 250 383 6864 ♦ fax: 812 355 4082

Dedication

For My Wife
Kathleen Lucille (Doheny) Tracey

For My Children
William Raymond Tracey, Jr.
Kevin Thomas Tracey
Brian John Tracey
Kathleen Lucille Bastille
Maura Gail Tarbania
Sean Michael Tracey

For My Grandchildren
Tamra Lee Letellier Lumpkin
Jacqueline Marie Munson
Michele Marie Coffman
Sean Keenan Letellier
Laine Tracey Tarbania
William Raymond Tracey III
Timothy Patrick Tracey
Kathleen Elizabeth Tracey
Victor Carrillo Tracey
Kolby Lynne Tracey
Kaylyn Michelle Tracey
Siara Carrillo Tracey

For My Great Grandchildren
Kaila Lee Lumpkin
Grace Marie Munson
David Matthew Munson

For My Friend and Companion
Else-Marie Birgit Bowe

Be calm and serene
Change your attitude toward life
By will and prayer

Contents

Grace is a first-rate
Relationship with your God
Cultivate that bond

Foreword

This book concludes the saga of the Tracey-O'Neill— the life and times of an Irish-French Canadian (with a smattering of American Indian, Spanish, and Swiss ancestors). When I completed the three earlier volumes of the trilogy, *Stands of Memory, Strands of Memory Revisited,* and *Strands of Memory Reprised,* I thought that I had exhausted the subject—that there was nothing left to write about. I was very wrong. I have remembered so many subjects, memories, incidents, and mental meanderings in the few years since their publication that I now have the contents of several additional books – but time and my advancing age will prevent the extension of this writing genre from continuing indefinitely. So this volume must be my swan song, rather than just an encore or curtain call. Regretfully, I have neither enough time nor the energy to undertake another volume.

Therefore, this book is a collection of poems, mainly free verse that I have written over the last few years. My hope is that some verses are insightful, but others are likely to be viewed as pedantic or mundane. Realistically, some poems are reasonably good verse and others may be mediocre. Nevertheless, all of them come from my heart. I make no apologies for that.

Some of the verses were written for Kathleen Lucille Tracey, my late spouse, lover. friend, and supporter for 56 wonderful years. Others were written for my children, grandchildren, great grandchildren, their spouses, other relatives, and my friends. More than a few verses were written for my lifeline, companion, and best friend for the last 11 years, Elsie-Marie Bowe. Still others were simply reflections and ruminations about life and the events that befall us mortals.

This series of anthologies is written primarily for my descendants — my children, grandchildren, great grandchildren—and for my cousins, nieces, nephews. and close friends. They are the people I love with all my heart and soul. My wife Kathleen made that point beautifully in a note she left in her own handwriting only a few months before she died. It read, "Love in your heart is not there to stay. Love is not love until you give it away!" She was so right!

All of the verses in this volume commemorate people who were very important in my life. Their love, friendship, support, courage, and strengths have been an inspiration to me. This verse is my way of memorializing them and sharing them with each other and the world.

Fortunately for me, poetry as an art form now allows writers to record their life experiences and share their poetic vision with others in a great variety of styles and forms, from more or less intricate rhyme schemes to free verse, a complete lack of rhyme. Although none of the poems in this collection involve complex rhyming, they include both verse in simple rhyming and straightforward narrative forms.

I know that these verses reveal more about William Raymond (O'Neill) Tracey than most men would like to have exposed to the view of others, particularly to the members of their extended family. But, I have always been a realist. I want my family and friends to know the real person that I am —my dreams, my fantasies, my weaknesses, my naiveté. So, there are very few things that remain hidden –and those are withheld only because I believe that they would be hurtful to others if revealed.

Putting my feelings and emotions into words and allowing my loved ones to experience with me the things that troubled, hurt, pleased, or delighted me, helped me to heal and made my life more meaningful and rewarding. Being able to express myself through the written word and share my thoughts and feelings with others are true blessings.

In summary, the verses that follow represent the distilled essence of my long life — impressions and visions that I hope will inspire readers at this point in their journey through life. I hope that they enjoy them.

I hope and pray that the people to whom this volume is dedicated will remember me with forbearance and love – as well as in their prayers. I also hope that they and those they love will have good health, happiness, and all of the things that will be useful to them in the plan of God.

With deepest respect and love to you all, from your Dad, Poppi, Abuelo, cousin, uncle, and friend, Bill.

William Raymond (O'Neill) Tracey

Make healthy choices
Practice moderation now
To enjoy good health

Love

There's a perfect match
For everyone in the world
Don't limit your search

Christmas with EMB 2011

It was almost a day
destined to be spent all alone.
Thanks to you, Else-Marie,
that didn't happen.

You are again a blessing to me,
as you have been such
for more than 10 years.
So today, Christmas Day,
we are together again,
with our families miles away.

There will be no decorations, Christmas tree,
or pile of colorfully wrapped presents.
However, there is one present for you,
which is enclosed with this verse.
The important thing is having your company
and the special repast.

We shall enjoy a traditional Christmas dinner:
medium rare roast prime beef,
with natural gravy, whipped potatoes
(with your portion removed before whipping),
two vegetables, green beans
and creamed onions, and
chocolate éclairs and ice cream for dessert

I also expect that we shall be receiving
many phone calls from our families.
But, the most important part of this celebration
is that we shall be together.

Origins of Love— An Enigma.

The sources of the attraction of two persons
to each other are almost infinite
in both kind and number.
However, they invariably involve
all of the senses:
touch, sight, hearing, taste, smell,
and, most of all the brain —
and its connection to human emotions,
sensibilities, experiences,
preferences, and attitudes.

All of these are unique to the individual.
That is why it is so often said
that there is a nearly perfect match
for everyone in the world —
in terms of race, color, height, weight,
appearance, sex or sexual orientation, intelligence,
personality, and just about every other
distinguishing trait or characteristic.

The challenge to every man and woman
is to find that person at the right time, place,
and under the right circumstances.

It is often true that the match-up
is not accepted
by those close to the couple involved.
A person is attracted to another in ways
and for reasons that are frequently
incomprehensible to others.

How can anyone explain why beautiful women
often choose plain (even ugly) men as their mates —
or why handsome men choose unattractive
(even homely) women as their lovers?
And why do brilliant men often choose
obviously feather-brained women as their consorts
—and bright women choose unlettered or not so
bright men as their lovers?

So eros arrives in unpredictable ways,
and that is the underlying reason for unlikely
yet long-lasting and very successful unions.

Sparkle

She reminds me of sparkle,
haphazardly, not systematically,
yet lovingly and tenderly,
her mind and attitude
glistening like a child's work of art.
She is my love and my companion,
the one who gave me
more than a decade of happiness
something I never expected.
Although the years have not always
been kind to either of us,
due to physical problems,
injuries, and other limitations,
they have not been incapacitating.
Her upbeat outlook and buoyant personality
have served as a model and standard
for me to duplicate.
I have tried to do just that —
and trust that I have done so.

Valentine's Day 2012

How lucky I was 11 years ago
when I walked through the Hallmark section
of Way's Center News
on my way to the parking lot.
I was stunned to see the lovely visage and figure
of a woman I had been admiring for several years
when I dropped off dry cleaning
at the South Yarmouth Acme Laundry.
She was Else-Marie Bowe, widowed
about a year earlier
by the death of her beloved husband, Clarence,
the victim of a heart attack.

I had become a widower in October 1997
when my dearly-loved wife Kathleen
died of a massive stroke.

Summoning up my courage,
I asked Else-Marie to consider having dinner
with me some evening
and asked for her phone number.
Without hesitation, she acquiesced.
That was the beginning of a loving relationship —
one that I never dreamed could come to pass.

Much has happened to EMB and me
in the intervening years:
dreaded diseases (breast, colon, and skin cancer),
serious accidents (broken hip), risky surgeries
(endarterectomy and hip replacement),
common conditions (hypertension and high cholesterol),
unexpected and unexplained disorders,

everyday ailments (colds and low back pain),
and that inevitable malady, aging.
One of the most striking contrasts
between us has been our reaction to adversity
in our physical condition and general health.
Elsie-Marie has invariably been upbeat,
uncomplaining, enduring, tolerating,
even accepting, of the worst medical
findings and prognoses.
She has handled them with equanimity
grace, and total self-control.
Bill Sr., in sharp and clear contrast,
after receiving negative medical news,
has typically been nonaccepting, irritable,
grouchy, dispirited, and depressed.
So, here's a resounding cheer
for a wonderful woman who,
for more than a decade,
has been an inspiration, model,
and standard for anyone who must face
and deal realistically with misfortune,
hardship, suffering, and adversity.
She has also been the great and true love
of my senior years —
a gift that I have neither earned nor deserve
but accept with heartfelt gratitude.

Haiku

Love is warm and kind
And also soul nourishing
Get it when you can

For Else-Marie On Her 71ˢᵗ Birthday

This is the second year of your seventieth decade.
I hope and pray that it will be
a better year for both of us.
The year 2011 has been a very difficult one,
not only for me, but also for you.
My visit to the Massachusetts General Hospital
for the left side endarterectomy in March
and the days that turned into weeks at the Cape Cod Hospital,
and the Spaulding Rehabilitation Hospital in August
for what was finally diagnosed as a seizure,
followed by the at-home rehab care
managed by the Visiting Nurse Association of Cape Cod,
at least in part, were due to my frustration
with my mental and physical conditions.
They were complicated, exacerbated, and intensified
by my six month driving proscription
and the unremitting visits of nurses, rehabilitation specialists,
as well as tradesmen and others to my home.
The result: a cantankerous, irritable, and difficult old man
with a short temper for you to have to deal with
and attempt to appease and pacify.
So, I am fortunate that you were able to bear with me
and make my life more comfortable and pleasant
than it would have been without your company —
and your comfort, assistance, nurturing,
support, and love.
To do all of that, and help by driving me to appointments,
making dump runs, shopping,
and waiting on me with drinking water,
medications, and other in-home services,
while working eight-hour shifts five days per week
at the Osterville Cumberland Farms convenience store,

were arduous. exhausting, and demanding jobs.
You are an amazing woman
and a blessing and joy to have in my life.
Thank you for being you!
HAPPY BIRTHDAY!

Love Letter

Writing a love letter
to my wife of three months,
sailing under the star-studded skies
in September 1944,
during the Second World War.
Feeling the moist air collecting on my skin
following a torrential rain storm
so common in the South Pacific.
Hearing the steady hum
of the twin Diesel engines,
and enduring their toxic fumes day and night
as we made our way North
from New Guinea to the Philippines.
Gazing at the greatest constellation
in the Southern Hemisphere
shining in the sea of stars —
the dazzling Southern Cross.
Asking for the protection of the Almighty
as we prepared to engage the enemy.
Drifting into the land of dreams
where I found my lovely young bride.
Remembering how difficult it was
to say goodbye to the love of my life,
not knowing whether we would
ever see each other again.

For Else-Marie on Her 72nd Birthday

Born on a Tuesday,
you share your birthday
with some very famous people:
Jodie Foster, child actress,
Calvin Klein, fashion designer
Ted Turner, founder of Turner Broadcasting
Dick Cavett, talk show host
Larry King, TV interviewer
Indira Gandhi, India's Prime Minister
Tommy Dorsey, Big Band leader
James Garfield, 20th U.S. President
It was that date in World War II—
when Adolph Hitler invaded Norway,
Denmark, the Netherlands,
Belgium, Luxembourg, and France;
Winston Churchill became
Prime Minister of Great Britain
Congress passed the Selective Training
and Service Act,
requiring drafting and training men
for the Army and Navy, Marines,
and National Guard.
You were completely oblivious
to those momentous events.
It was just as well that you were.
But, you survived the war
and lived to emigrate to the United States
where we worked together in 2002
to achieve your US citizenship.
You are so bright and self-sufficient,
so capable and competent
and so thoughtful and loving.

When my wife Kathleen died,
I became morose, depressed, and miserable.
I fully expected to remain in that state
for the rest of my life.
I never expected to find someone
to fill that great void in my life —
give me purpose and fulfillment.
You were one who offered me
new life and love.
It was and is a very precious gift.
one that I had neither deserved nor earned.
But, I accepted it willingly and wholeheartedly.
So, thank you for the last decade.
I wish I could have ten more years,
but that is asking too much.
I also know that there are too many times
when I am grouchy, short-tempered, and impatient.
Those unfortunately are all too often the hallmarks
of the octogenarian and the nonagenarian.
I also believe that it is what it is.
Thank you for your forbearance and understanding,
but most of all for your devotion and love.
HAPPY BIRTHDAY

Haiku

Remember this truth
Happiness lies in the heart
Not in the venue

Grace is a first-rate
Relationship with your God.
Cultivate that bond.

Verse from the Heart

She was a near-perfect woman,
about as close to flawless
as any woman can be.
He was like a carnation,
one whose sensibilities
and responsiveness unfolded
as he got to know her over time –
with intriguing tales of then
in Germany and now
in the United States.
Radiant light danced in her crinkled
and well-lived eyes
eye-lids fluttering with care and refinement.
I gave her a verse that I had written
to celebrate our time together
and commented, "You inspired me to write this.
It's mediocre because it does not do justice
to the loving relationship we have."
She took my hand in hers and replied,
"I'm confident that it does
because it comes from your heart."
She was right!

Haiku

Verse is just one way
Of saying that I love you
Accept it for that

Family

The center of life
Is a loving family
Earned, never issued

For Grace on Her 5th Birthday

I wish that I could be with you
on this important day in your young life.
In fact, I wish that I could have been with you
on all of your other birthdays.

A distance far too long separates us.
But that doesn't mean
that I don't think of you often
and pray for you every night
just before I go to sleep.

I hope to see you here on Cape Cod soon.
I find it difficult to believe
that so many years have passed —
and that you are now FIVE years old —
a very bright, lovely, and loving young lady!

Here are my feelings
in Haiku, Japanese verse
On your special day

You're my great grandchild
A grand gift in a long life
One to be treasured

Three essential traits
For success in your lifetime
Smarts, grace, and wisdom

What I wish for you
My beautiful Grace Marie
Are good health and bliss

For Victor On His 13th Birthday

Congratulations! You are now a teenager —
customarily defined as a boy or girl
between the ages of 13 and 19
or numerical ages ending in "teen"
— and otherwise known as
a teen or teener, an adolescent,
a juvenile, a pubescent, a minor —
or in less complimentary terms,
as a "teenybopper,."
So, in another eight years
you will become an adult,
with all the responsibilities
that accrue to that exalted status.
My unsolicited but sound advice follows.
It is phrased in Haiku,
a Japanese form of poetry
that must have only three lines
with lines 1, 2, and 3
requiring 5, 7, and 5 syllables, respectively.
Here it is:

Three essential traits
For success in any field
Smarts, grace, and wisdom

Remember this truth
Happiness lies in the heart
Not in the venue

The sweetest revenge
Is to forgive the doer
With a heartfelt smile

All that we now have
Emanates from our God's hand
We have to share it

What I wish for you
Victor Carrillo Tracey
Is the very best.

Written with admiration, high hopes,
much love; and many prayers.
HAPPY BIRTHDAY!

The Tracey Brothers

Guardian Angels protecting,
guiding, and always
watching each other's backs.
Do they ever disagree
argue, or fight?
Of course.
They are boys,
and that's what boys do.
Brothers they are and always there,
with laughter, love, and care.
However, Bill Jr, Kevin,
Brian, and Sean
are often smiling
just because they are brothers,
and they are often laughing
because here's nothing
you, me, or anyone else
can do about it!

My Family

Family has always meant everything to me.
My history made my brothers and sisters
the center of my life.
My mother died in childbirth
when my sister Eileen was born.
I was only 16 months old.
On that sad day. my baby sister and I were separated from my
sisters Mary, Pauline, and Margaret, and my brother James
when my Aunt Josephine,
my mother's sister, responded to my mother's request
and took us home to Leominster to live with her
and her husband, Eddie,
and care for us as if we were her own.
Meanwhile, my siblings were parceled out to grandparents
and other aunts until my Dad made arrangements with two
orphanages, operated by nuns
in Leicester and Worcester, for Jim and the three girls.
They remained there until my Dad remarried a few years later,
built a home across the street
from where Eileen and I were living,
and brought our siblings home to live near us.
So, although we did not live together,
we attended the same school and saw each other daily.
That continued for about five years,
while dad made weekly rounds to visit all his children and Aunt
Josephine made sure that Eileen and I visited our sisters and
brother at the orphanages often.
Following the birth of my half-brothers,
Francis and John, until that part of the family
moved to Brookline.
Although my dad wanted to take me with them,
And I, at about age six, was asked

to make the choice — go with Dad to Boston
or stay with the only mother I had ever known.
In the end, I did not have to choose
because my Dad's new wife Sarah,
refused to take me because she had more children
than she could handle.

Sisters, Friends Forever
Good sisters are sometimes rare.
Kathy and Maura are examples
of the ideal sibling rapport —
sisters who treasure and care.
Although they sometimes disagree,
the sisters in the Tracey clan
are a special breed
because they are now and forever
clearly and conspicuously family.
And that's precisely the way it ought to be!

Your Mother
Never forget these words
because they truly describe
the origin, role, and importance
of the greatest gift every
man, woman, and child have received.
*****

There is but one and only one,
whose love will fail you never
One who lives from sun to sun,
with constant fond endeavor.
There is but one and only one,
on earth there is no other,
In heaven a noble work was done
when God gave you a Mother.

For Bill Jr. on His 65th Birthday

Congratulations! You have just joined
a fast-growing club —
the Social Security/Medicare club,
recipients of the Fed's largess.
The so-called "Golden Years"
are not all that they are purported
or advertised to be.
Maybe for a few lucky ones,
they are truly wonderful years.
But for the great majority of "elders,"
those years mean
more frequent visits to physicians,
higher healthcare costs,
an ever-enlarging home pharmacy,
less sharp vision and greater hearing loss,
more restrictions on their activities,
new and daily aches and pains,
and other examples of physical deterioration
that are better left unmentioned.
Of course there are some exceptions
to the latter, with regard to which
we are both blessed
with some important exceptions.
But before leaving this list of ills,
let us not forget
the increase in short-term memory loss
(names and misplaced objects
confounded or complemented by
clear recollections of people
and events of long ago).
And, at the same time,
facing daily more and more people,

including family, relatives, friends,
fellow workers, and casual acquaintances,
who demonstrate by their questions and actions,
that they wonder whether we still
"have all of our marbles"
or are beginning to show
the onset of dementia.
Let me turn now to the positives
about your personal attributes
and your challenging and interesting life
from a father's perspective covering
65 years of observation:
You were a beautiful blonde baby,
although burdened by colic;
a handsome and precocious child,
described by doctors
at the Boston Children's Hospital
as a budding genius;
and a very inquisitive youngster.
You were always asking, What's that?
How does it work? Can I have it?
Can I play with it?
You were a good pupil in grade school,
although things came so easily to you
that you could not be bothered with homework.
You were by choice (and unknown
until after the fact
by your Mom and Dad)
an intermittent or frequent truant
student in high school and college,
but you did receive
your high school diploma and an associate degree.
You were largely a self-taught
clarinetist and saxophonist

and a very good vocalist.
You served your country
with honor and bravery in Vietnam.
You were and are a talented videographer
and editor, lighting and sound expert,
and jack-of-all-trades.
You are a talented cook
of meat and poultry— roasts, chops, and steaks,
and seafood,
including lobsters, and more exotic meals—
whether using a stove or a grille.
You are a great builder and fixer-upper
taking on jobs from electronics to carpentry,
electrical work, plumbing, and masonry.
You have proved yourself to be a loving
and dedicated father to LB, Tim, and Katie.
With your early suitor activities,
(unknown to me except Thu)
and more recent lady-friends Jay, Kim, and Suzanne
and two marriages (Lynda and Kathy),
you have proved yourself to be a "ladies' man
par excellence,"
a lover, a Lothario or Don Juan,
who must always have a "lady love" at his side.
You have more company in that respect
among family, friends, and acquaintances
than you know.
Good luck and best wishes in your winter years.

Haiku

Days are all too short
Enjoy the small things in life
Love yourself today

My Sister, Mary Josephine

The oldest in the O'Neill family of six,
Mary was born in Roxbury, MA August 1, 1916.
She worked for the federal government as a secretary
in Springfield. MA and then in Washington, DC
from age 18 until she married Robert Kirby
of Leominster on November 30, 1946.
She died in childbirth September 27, 1947
and was buried with her daughter, Patricia Ann,
in St. Leo's Cemetery in Leominster.
Mary was a warm, caring, and generous young woman
who was especially good to her younger brother.
When she came home to Leominster,
she never failed to visit me
and bring me small presents.
When I was 16, she took me on my first trip
to New York City, where we toured
Radio City, saw the Rockettes,
ate at the Automat, Jack Dempsey's restaurant
(and shook hands with the champion boxer),
and Toffinetti's on Times Square,
visited Grant's tomb, the Empire State Building,
and climbed the Statue of Liberty
all the way to the top of the torch —
and were televised in black and white
in a demonstration somewhere in Radio City.
Mary was my favorite sister. I miss her very much.

Haiku
Take the time to live
Feel the warm sun on your face
You'll look much better

For Unidentified Loved Ones

You probably didn't notice
that I did not compose a verse
nor send you a check
for your last birthday.
However, that was not due
to the failing memory of your
nonagenarian relative.
Rather it was a penalty
for your failure to acknowledge
those mementoes on your birthday.
As I reminded all of you
a few years ago,
I expend a considerable amount
of thought, time, energy, and love
writing verses—and sending checks.
A short, hand-written note,
E-mail, or phone call
of thanks is not only proper
but also an obligation of the recipient
of such gifts.
I did not have the heart
to deny gifts to you
for the last two Christmases —
despite the lack of thank you notes.
In the future, I may not
make the same mistake.
So, this could be the last of my gifts
on the occasions of your birthdays
and Christmases.
I leave this missive with deep regret,
my heart-felt prayers, best wishes,

and this Irish Blessing:
May God be with you and Bless you.
May you be poor in misfortunes
and rich in blessings.
May you know nothing but happiness
from this day forward.

My Brother, James Edward

Jim was born in Roxbury, MA on August 6, 1917.
When we lived across the street from each other in Leominster.
Jim recruited me to be a helper with his newspaper route
very early every morning on the West Side of town.
Following his Army Air Corps service as a radioman
in Italy and Liberia and Spanish Morocco in Africa,
Jim worked as a salesman for the *Catholic Digest*
and later as publisher and editor of *Boston Today*
and *New England Today* magazines.
Jim married Mary Therese (Terri) Mannix
November 23, `1953 — I served as best man.
Jim and Terri had one child, Christine Ann, my Godchild.
Before he married, Jim spent most of his weekends visiting
Kathleen and me in Leominster, Fitchburg, and Ashby—
and taking me (and sometimes Kathleen) on long trips
in his 1936 Chevrolet to New York City, Pittsburg,
Washington, DC, Toronto, and Montreal.
After Jim married, we saw each other infrequently
until he retired, having suffered heart attacks, strokes.
a quadruple heart bypass, and kidney cancer.
Jim was an after midnight talk show caller,
becoming famous as Boston's "Chauncey."
I recorded, edited, and published his memoirs,
The Indomitable O'Neill. I miss him very much

For Jackie M. on Her 35th Birthday

The year was 1976, a Leap Year.
Gerald R. Ford was President
and Nelson D. Rockefeller was VP.
Jimmy Carter was elected President Nov 2nd.
The Boston Celtics won the NBA title.
The Grammy Awards that year were:
Recording — *Love Will Keep Us Together*
Song of the Year — *Send in the Clowns*
Life expectancy was 72.9 years
Median household income was $12,686
and a 1st class stamp cost 13 cents.
But the most important event for you,
your parents, and your grandparents, was your birth,
at the Leominster Hospital.
A lot of things have happened to all of us
in the intervening years —
including the births of your sister, Mikie.
and ten cousins —
and the acquisition and departure
of six temporary aunts and three uncles.
The important point is that
the Tracey Family remains strong
simply because God made us a special family.
We need each other. We love one another
and forgive one another.
We work together and play together.
Side by side and arm in arm, we grow in God's love
and learn to love all men, women, and children.
Together we serve our Maker and seek to know His will.
These are our hopes and ideals.
Lord, we ask for the grace to attain them.
May God bless us all on this special day

with this unique Irish blessing:
May all of our blessings outnumber
the shamrocks that grow.
And may troubles avoid us
wherever we go.
HAPPY BIRTHDAY!

My Sister, Pauline Rita

Polly, .the third O'Neill child and second girl,
was born in Brookline, November 12, 1918.
She was beautiful—dark auburn hair and blue eyes.
Polly worked as a receptionist for a prominent
law firm in Boston for many years.
She married John K. Kidik, January 19, 1939.
John was a rigger in a Boston shipyard,
and later worked at U.S. Steel as a crane operator.
They had one child, daughter Barbara Dolores.
Barbara never contacted any member of the O'Neill
Family following Polly's death in late 1970.
Polly was a warm-hearted, fun-loving woman
who spread joy wherever she went.
The Kidiks lived in the Mission Hill Project,
which we visited for many years — including
Kathleen and my honeymoon where,
due to lack of funds,
we spent four nights in Barbara's bed
before I left for the War in the Pacific.
Polly lived in Needham with her daughter
until she died of a heart problem.
I miss her terribly.

For Lina on Her 44th Birthday

This is another auspicious day for you,
Sean, Victor, and Siara—
and now for me too!
For many years it been my privilege
to call you my daughter-in-law.
And I do that with great pride
and thanks for the happy and loving relationship
between you and my talented
and accomplished youngest son, Sean —
as well as for your superlative parenting
of my wonderful and loving grandchildren.
Here is my prayer for my caring
and devoted daughter-in-law
and her family:
Lord, bless my daughter-in-law
and the family that I love.
Comfort them each day
as daytime turns to nighttime,
please bring them peace, I Pray.
When morning comes tomorrow,
let all their cares be small.
Guide them with your wisdom,
Lord, bless them one and all.
HAPPY BIRTHDAY

Haiku

What I wish for you
Lina Carrillo Tracey
The best life offers.

My Sister, Margaret Elizabeth

Peg was born in Brookline May 26, 1920.
She was a blonde blue-eyed girl, close in visage
complexion, and demeanor to me.
She married Francis C. DiPietrantonio Sept. 15, 1940.
Their first child, Elizabeth Ann, died (crib death)
at age three months on February 23, 1944.
Peg and Frank had a son, Francis, in 1944.
Frank Sr. died of leukemia January 27, 1949.
Peg remained a widow for 24 years,
serving as a teller in a Boston bank.
She then married Joseph Natale (Frank's cousin).
Joe died of lung cancer in 1983.
Peg and Frank remained in their Needham home
until Peg died July 10, 2010.
Frank Jr. never married—
instead he served as his mother's companion
and caretaker for the rest of her life.
Peg was a regular guest at the Tracey's, attending holiday
celebrations, and parties at our homes in Ashby,
and Townsend, family get-togethers at Bill Jr.'s and Kevin's
in Manchester and Goffstown, and the annual Memorial Mass,
cemetery visitation, and family dinner
for Kathleen on Cape Cod.
Until Peg died, July 10, 2010, Frank attended all the events.
Since then, despite frequent phone calls and letters,
I have heard nothing from him
despite the promise he made
at his mother's funeral to keep in touch with me.
I am disheartened and desolated
by this state of affairs.

For Kathy B. on Her Birthday

Today I'm appreciating you
for all the happiness you've brought me
through the years,
for all the strengths and fortitude you have
and the caring and love you have returned.
Thank you for all that you are,
my wonderful, gifted, and loving daughter.
It is natural for you to say something cheerful.
to do something thoughtful
to be the special daughter you are.
So, this birthday verse is not just
an expression of my heart-felt birthday wishes.
Sometimes I just sit, remember, smile, and feel happy
there are people like you in the world.
You, your brothers and sister,
my grandchildren and great grandchildren
have made my world such a wonderful place to be.
It takes such thoughtfulness and caring
to be the daughter you are.
So, there's a special place within my heart
that's meant for you alone —
a special place within my heart
reserved for times we've known —
especially in Ashby and Townsend
when a little girl late at night
slipped downstairs to spend some time
sitting in a rocking chair with her Daddy.
Your birthday is also a celebration
of the superb daughter you are
and for all the days, past, present, and future,
that you have been and will always be a part of my life.
May good health and happiness touch your life

as warmly and consistently
as your caring has touched mine.
I close with this Irish Prayer:
May your thoughts be as glad as the shamrocks,
May your heart be as light as a song.
May each day bring you bright happy hours,
That stay with you all the year long.

For My Daughters

An Angel visited me one March day
and came again on a September revisit
four years later.
In either case I don't think I was ready,
but I don't believe that I would have it
any other way.
One little Angel arrived
with dark hair and eyes
the other a blond with eyes
as bright as the skies.
Upon first seeing each one
in the Lucy Helen hospital nursery room,
I whispered, "I love you,"
as I silently cried,
the tears falling slowly from my eyes.
Those tiny Angel faces
with the look of innocence
that nothing could erase,
stole my heart away
on those March and September days.
I will love them both until the day I die
and the eons thereafter wherever I lie.
Then with the other Angels in Heaven
we shall forever reside.

For Kaylyn on Her 12th Birthday

Born on a Tuesday. a Leap Year,
the first year of the 21st Century,
and the first year of the term of office of
William (Bill) Jefferson Clinton
the forty-second President of the United States.
It was also the year that Hillary Rodham Clinton
was elected the junior New York Senator;
of foolish fears that Y2K's computers
would not shift from 1999 to 2000 correctly,
that Playstation 2 was released,
and that Dora the Explorer,
one of Nickelodeon's hottest shows, debuted.
Here are some average costs in 2000:
new house $134,150; one month's rent $675;
yearly income $40,343; new car $24,750;
and a postage stamp 33 cents.
Popular musicians: U2, Red Hot Chile Peppers,
Madonna, Bon Jovi, and Britney Spears.
But, this verse is for and about you, my beautiful
and exceptionally gifted granddaughter,
and your Nanni's seventh granddaughter.
It's a shame that she did not live to see you
become the lovely young woman that you are.
But I know that she is watching over you and Kolby
with much love and great pride.
Here is one of her favorite Irish prayers—
one that she would offer up for you
— as I do now:
May you live a long life
Full of gladness and health
With a pocket full of gold
As the least of your wealth,

May the dreams you hold dearest,
Be those that come true,
The love that you spread,
Keep returning to you.
HAPPY BIRTHDAY

My Sister, Eileen Ann

Eileen was my closest sister because we lived together
with our Aunt Josephine and Unclc Eddie Tracey —
who, in 1940 became our foster parents
when we were adopted.
Eileen was Pop's favorite while I was resented.
Nevertheless, Pop supported me until I finished high school.
Eileen was a very bright girl, and, seeing no need to study,
made it through high school with no problems.
She worked at the Cluett Peabody Shirt Factory
as a sewing machine piecework operator.
She married a soldier, Edward J. Hendershaw
of New York City January 29, 1942.
Eileen and Eddie had three sons,
Edward Jr., James, and Scott.
When she stopped working, she developed and practiced
the hobby of home buying, refurnishing, and selling
properties in Leominster, Fitchburg, Lunenburg,
Cape Cod, and even Escondido, California.
After returning to Leominster, Eddie became involved
in the Elks, ultimately becoming the Exalted Ruler
of the Leominster Lodge.
Eddie moved to Escondido, a few years
after Eileen died during heart bypass surgery April 26,1983
to be near his sons.
I have not heard from him since,
although I have tried to contact him.

For Steve

About three years have passed
since I first met Maura's friend, Steve,
a quiet man, but one with evident class.
The intervening years have elapsed
with stunning changes
in the nature and depth of their relationship.
It has evolved from friendship
to romance.
And, although not the business
of observers, including close relatives, and me,
the transformation is of primary import
to its participants.

As one whose primary concern
is the welfare and happiness
of my daughter, I m pleased to report
that I am completely delighted
with this turn of events.
My conclusion is that Steve
and my Maura have mystically connected.
They take unmistakable pleasure
and fulfillment in their being together.
It is nothing short of magical.

Steve has amply demonstrated his considerable talents:
jack of all trades, computer trouble shooter,
electronics wizard, skilled plumber, electrician.
and painter, able window caulker, lawn
and garden specialist—and a host of other jobs.
You name the job, and Steve can handle it
promptly and skillfully.

He is also an gustatory connoisseur
with a surprising capacity
considering his size and weight
but attributable to his adherence
to a challenging workout regimen.
He is surprisingly fond of plain milk,
which he consumes with gusto, pleasure, and bliss.
He is also amenable to gastronomic experimentation,
willing to try just about anything,
including exotic fare —and ("pretend"?) to enjoy it.

Steve also has a well-cultivated sense of humor
and is a good conversationalist.
But, most important of all
are Steve's sterling personal qualities:
he is bright, articulate, thoughtful, humble,
considerate, patient, and loving.
In short Steve is a Good man,
one whom I endorse without reservation
— and also count as my friend.

Haiku for Steve

What I wish for you
Stephen P. Mottley and san
The best life offers.

An analog man
In today's digital world
A bad place to be

The key to long life
Stay positive in outlook
Don't sweat the small stuff

My Brother, Francis Xavier

My brother Frank, FX as he was known,
was my Dad's first son
with Sarah (Sally McNamara) O'Neill.
Born in Leominster July 3, 1932,
Frank was a bright, good-humored, funny,
and out-going redhead and talented athlete —
a Massachusetts Junior Tennis champion
and a low-handicap golfer.
He married Margaret Nelson May 31, 1958.
They had four children: Kathleen,
Karen, James, and Mark.
Frank was an outstanding salesman
and later a buyer for Mr. Donut and S.S. Pierce.
Frank died of cancer (melanoma)
on September 29, 1982, only four months
after the cancer was detected.
He as an occasional over-night visitor to our home
on the Cape with his wife, Peg.
Although we did not see each other often,
except for weddings and such,
we were close friends. I miss him very much.

Haiku for FX

Increase your golf score
And add to your handicap
By catching the yips

Hit it where they ain't
That's the goal of the batter
And the way to win

For Dennis

Garrulous and loquacious,
Dennis is invariably irrepressible,
and, at the same time, consistently affable,
welcoming, genial, sociable, and amiable.
He is also widely renowned
as a copious consumer of Diet Coke —
and more notably
as a consummate epicure, gastronome,
and connoisseur of food of all kinds
from appetizers and fast foods
to full dinners of roasts, steaks, and chops—
which he consumes with gusto and enjoyment.
Ever a bike enthusiast,
Dennis is the proud owner of five
motor cycles at his home in Hollis,
and one at his condo on the island of Kauai, Hawaii.
He also takes great delight in cycle trips
along New Hampshire's twisting secondary roads
to its popular beaches and seacoast city of Portsmouth —
with Kathy holding on tightly behind him.
An accomplished "fixer-upper,"
he keeps his equipment in top shape
and his property well manicured — although at times
with the help of his landscaper stepson, Sean.
Dennis has proved to be a loving
and exceptional stepfather to Sean and Tamra
and an outstanding and doting grandfather to Kaila.
Dennis will always be remembered
by hundreds of children of all ages
as their guardian and friend while, for countless years,
he served as a school crossing guard.
My son-in-law Dennis is THE MAN and a GOOD ONE!

For Kevin and Brian on Their 64th Birthday

Unbelievable! My twin sons
are only one year away
from collecting their monthly
Social Security checks!
Strangely enough,
the twins are as different in as many ways
as they are identical—which, over the years,
has caused me and others
conniption fits,
notional or hypothetical paroxysms.
How are they alike?
In looks, although often
varying in weight, hairstyles, and demeanor,
they both exhibit optimism,
self-confidence, and determination,
complemented by fortitude.
And they are both lovers par excellence,
in my view, totally without
equals, challengers, or rivals—
in a word, masters of the art
of conquest, even if not permanent.
For example, Kevin's history
includes four divorces —
while Brian has none.
Nonetheless, they are connoisseurs
of captivating, striking,
seductive, and fascinating women,
Brian's Joanne,
and Kevin' new wife, Lin Li.
For years, Kevin, Brian, and brother Bill Jr.
had a very popular show band
called "The Prodigy."

The choice of title was fortuitous,
as well as prophetic, even visionary.
Kevin is noted for being a prodigious
progenitor of lovely progeny—
Kolby and Kaylyn.
And Brian is known for being the
impressive originator of beautiful offspring—
Jackie and her bright and talented children,
Grace and David,
and his stunning and highly successful
entrepreneurial daughter, Mikie.
Both of the twins have hearty appetites
for opulence — and the "good life" —
in terms of luxurious and tasteful
homes and vacation property,
lavish and state of the art "boy's toys"
— for Kevin, twin engine, high altitude
airplanes and luxurious cars —
and for Brian, large (sail) yachts
and (Harley) motorcycles.
I am proud of my children,
all six of them,
and each one is different in some respect.
I cherish those differences,
which resulted in some of my most memorable
paternal experiences,
ones that I shall never forget.
Many of them are described in my memoirs
and in the four *Strands of Memory* anthologies.
I close with their mother's
maxim and dictum:
Love is not love until you give it away.

For Frank DiPietrantonio

Your Uncle Bill is distraught,
troubled, and distressed,
as well as perplexed, confused, and mystified,
by your failure to reply to his letters of entreaty,
invitations to visit and attend
the anniversary Mass and dinner,
and his inability to contact you
by phone for more than two years.
All this despite your promise
at your mother's funeral to "keep in touch."
I believe that you have been undergoing
serious problems with your vision,
but I regret that you did not deem it necessary
to keep me informed of your condition.
I, too, have had two very bad years,
involving risky surgery, rehabilitation,
problems with my vision, hearing, balance,
and feelings of malaise, as I enter my 90th year.
I hope and pray that you will contact me
to set right whatever is wrong with our relationship
before it is too late,
I close with this Irish verse
about our extended family:
God made us a family. We need and love each other
and forgive one another.
We work and play together. We worship together
and use God's Word together.
Together we grow in Christ and learn to love all men.
Together we serve our God
and seek to know His will. These are our hopes and ideals.
Lord, we ask for the grace to attain them.

For Kolby on Her 14th Birthday

Born on a Thursday,
you share your birthday
with some very famous people:
Mary Higgins Clark, novelist
Ricky Martin, pop singer
Ava Gardner, actress
Howard Hughes, aviation millionaire.
I can hardly believe how much
prices have changed since 1998!
In that year, these were the averages:
A new home $129,300, Annual income $38,100
Monthly rent $619, Gallon of gas $1.15
But, this verse is about Kolby,
my lovely and talented granddaughter.
It's difficult for me to believe
that you are now 14 years of age —
no longer a child, but now a young woman!
Where did all of those years go?
Obviously they were well spent
because they produced
a very mature, stunning, gifted,
warm, and loving young woman,
one of whom I am very proud.
I wish you the best that life has to offer
in the years to come.
In the words of an old Irish blessing:
May God be with you and bless you.
May you see your children's children.
May you be poor in misfortune
and rich in blessings.
May you know nothing but happiness
from this day forward.

For Sean L. on His 34th Birthday

Born on a Tuesday
during the presidency of Jimmy Carter
and the election of John Paul II as the 264th Pope.
It was also the year of the Great New England Blizzard
that killed 100 people and caused $520M in damage
However, this is another milestone in your life,
simply because life insurance actuaries
estimate that on average you have lived about one third
of the years you were allotted at birth.
Here are some fascinating facts about 1978.
Average costs that year:
A new house $54,000   Personal Income $17,000
One month's rent $200   Gallon of gasoline 63 cents
Popular musicians and songs that year
The Bee Gees: "*Night Fever*" and "*Stay'in Alive*"
Rolling Stones: "*Hot Rocks*," and "*Exile on Main Street*
Commodores: "*Three Times a Lady*" and "*Only You.*"
You share a birthday with Johann Sebastian Bach,
composer and musician,
and Matthew Broderick, two-time Tony Award winner.
But, this verse is about you, my first grandson,
and your Nanni's favorite and first grandson.
It's a shame that she did not live to see you
become the fine man that that you have become.
But I know that she is watching over you and Leah
with much love and great pride.
Here is her favorite Irish prayer—
one that she would offer up for you — as I do now:
May God's Holy Wisdom and Infinite Love
Look down on you always from Heaven above
May God send you good fortune, contentment, and peace
And may all of your blessings forever increase.

For Jackie M. on Her 36th Birthday

Born on a Sunday,
during the 200th birthday of the United States,
you share your birthday with some very famous people:
Reese Witherspoon, actress
Tracy Austin. tennis champion
Cathy Rigsby, Olympic gymnast
Connie Francis, vocalist
(*"Who's Sorry Now"*)
How costs have changed since 1976:
Average new house $43,400
Average annual income $16,000
Gallon of gas 59 cents
But, this verse is about you,
my lovely granddaughter,
wife of Matthew, and mother
of my great grandchildren
Grace and David.
The older I get (I'm in my 90th year)
the longer the interval of time
since you and your family moved to Seattle
and the less frequent the opportunities to see you
and my great grandchildren.
Although you have been good about sending me photos,
I have only seen Grace once, and I have yet to meet David.
I hope and pray that I can hold them
in my arms at least once before I move on.
Meanwhile, I hope and pray
that all is well with you and your family.
I close with this Irish blessing:
May your troubles be less, and your blessings be more
And nothing but happiness, come through your door.

For Siara on Her 11th Birthday

Recently, your Aunt Kathy told me
that she saw you starring as Charlie Bucket
in the play "Charlie and the Chocolate Factory,"
demonstrating your talent as an actress.
I'm not surprised, but I am very pleased.
Do you know that you share a birthday
with two famous actresses?
They are Barbara Stanwyck, nominated four times
for an Academy Award and winner
of three Emmy Awards and a Golden Globe —
and Ginger Rogers, Academy Award winner,
singer, and dance partner of the famous Fred Astaire.
But, this bit of verse is for and about you.
My unsolicited advice follows.
It is phrased in Haiku, a Japanese form of poetry.

Enjoy "small" things now
The "big" things will come later
Face them at that time

Do your very best
Even when no one watches
That marks true greatness

Understand this truth
You're better than you believe
Enjoy your blessings

My prayer for you:
A long, hale, and happy life
Truly lacking strife

For Mikie on Her 33rd Birthday

Today is another milestone in your life.
Born on a Monday,
you share your birthday with Jennifer Page,
singer-songwriter (1998 pop hit "Crush")
and Michele Hiltz, American film and TV actress.
During the year of your birth,
Jimmy Carter was President, and
Margaret Thatcher was elected UK Prime Minister.
The average cost of a home was $17,500,
monthly rent was $280,
average income was $17,500,
and a gallon of gasoline cost 86 cents.
The most popular musicians and songs were
"Love You Inside Out" – Bee Gees
"Heart of Glass" — Blondie
"Bad Girls" — Donna Summer.
But this is about you —
my beautiful granddaughter.
I hope that all is well with you
and especially your love life.
I know that you are doing
a superb job with Ride the Ducks of Seattle,
but there is much more to life than work.
Remember this:
To your Poppi. you will always be loved,
Not only for the smiling little girl
that hugged me whenever we met,
but also for the kindhearted way
that as an adult you live,
And you will always be wished
joyful days in return
for the warm-hearted happiness that you give.

For David on His 2nd Birthday

Today you are age two,
and I have yet to see or meet you!
Of course I have received photos
of my only great grandson,
but I still want to see you and hold you in my arms
before that is no longer possible.
Regardless of that fact, I want you to know
that your great grandfather loves you
and deeply regrets that he never
had the opportunity to be with you,
talk to you, and play with you.
I also want you to know
that your great grandmother, Kathleen,
knows you and loves you
from her place in Heaven,
watches over you, and protects you from harm.
How she misses holding
and hugging you and your sister, Grace!
So, David, remember that we love you,
wish you a happy birthday,
and will be watching you
celebrate this one and those that will follow.
I close this verse with an Irish blessing:
As Saint Patrick brought new faith to Ireland,
so may he bring to you,
a touch of Irish happiness in everything you do.
And, like the good Saint Patrick,
may your family, home, and life be blessed
with all God's special favors
that will make you happiest.

For Victor on His 14ᵗʰ Birthday

Born on a Friday in 1998,
you share your birthday
with some very famous people:
Joseph Biden, VP of the United States
Alistair Cooke, journalist
James M. Curley, 4-time Mayor of Boston
Edwin Hubble, astronomer
But this verse is about you,
my talented and personable grandson,
one for whom I predict
a very bright life of accomplishments.
What will that require
in addition to your God-given gifts?
I turn to Kaifu to identify some key imperatives:

Trust your gut feelings
Avoid procrastination
Get it done right now!

Despite importance
Whenever you are involved
Do your very best

When you get it wrong
Don't ever punish yourself
Simply make it right

I close with this old Irish proverb:
Before you go to bed,
give your troubles to God.
He will be up all night anyway.

For Lin Li on Her Engagement

Lin Li is an example and model
of the ideal Asian young woman:
slender, vibrant, gracious. and eye-catching
in looks, manner, shape, form,
and the timbre and quality of her voice.
She epitomizes female loveliness,
regardless of race, nationality, and any other
attribute or characteristic.
Lin is so "knowing" —
articulate, sagacious, artful, astute, foxy,
perceptive, shrewd, sharp-witted.
bright, and insightful —
in the presence of men and women,
young or old, married or single, gay or straight,
smart or dense, or in between on all counts.
This captivating creature with striking jet-black hair,
enthralling almond eyes, and alluring ivory skin,
will exchange vows with my second son, Kevin,
at their wedding in early September.
This relationship demonstrates yet again
that there are people who do not understand
the genesis and complexities of love
and remain unconvinced of the sincerity
of the love, two who differ on some characteristic,
have for each other.
Here, the disparity in their ages is the primary concern
of those who have reservations
about the wisdom of the relationship.
Lin is in the "early summer" of her life,
and Kevin is in the "early winter" of his—
reflecting my concept of the seasons of life:
spring encompasses ages 12 to 20, summer ages 21 to 40,

fall ages 41 to 60, and winter ages 61 to 85+.
I wish you and Kevin the very best life offers
and close with this Irish prayer:
May you be blessed always with a sunbeam to warm you,
a moonbeam to charm you, and a sheltering angel
so nothing can harm you.

Attributes of a Woman "Friend"

Whenever I hear the words "woman friend,"
or even think about women,
I focus on their most endearing qualities,
whether they are girls, maidens,
misses, lassies, or ladies,
young or old, single or married,
gay or straight.
I think of their soft skin,
silken hair, and velvety lips,
shapely breasts, buttocks, and legs,
bright and radiant eyes,
white teeth and winning smiles.
I also think about inviting glances,
pleasing voices and musical laughter,
welcoming hugs, and comforting hands,
reassuring words, and tender kisses.
Of course, I also think of the scent of perfume,
the painted fingernails and toenails—
sometimes even the silk lingerie.
But most of all, I think of
their femininity in total,
their warmth and kindness,
and their response and reaction to me.

For Kevin and Brian On Their 63rd Birthday

Although I don't have the smarts or writing skills
that until recently I owned,
I would be remiss if I failed to memorialize
your sixty-third birthday in verse.
So, here goes my best effort to do so.
*****

Your birth was of signal importance
to your Mom and me, to your brother, Bill,
to your unborn siblings, your grandparents,
and other relatives and friends,
if not to the rest of the world!
Your births also profoundly changed my life
as well as your mother's.
*****

Surprisingly, your imminent arrival
was not predicted until about ten days
before your birth.
So, instead of expecting a very large baby,
we got two 5+ pound infants!
*****

As a consequence, we had to make some
important purchases and adjustments —
double just about everything—
diapers and bottles,
formula and rocking chairs,
binkies and blankets,
and later,
bassinets and cribs,
carriages and walkers,
and time for rocking, cuddling, and loving.
But, we also had to cut other things in half —
hours of uninterrupted sleep for us,

time for ourselves,
our budget for movies, restaurant dinners,
entertainment and hobbies,
and for visiting friends and relatives.
But, the changes also resulted in the multiplication
of our love for our children and for each other,
a love that continued to grow as we aged.
We also had to deal with the clichés about twins
and the dumb questions
people invariably ask about them,
many answers to which were either obvious or unanswerable.
*****

In summary, the experience of having and rearing twins
has been interesting, exciting, and challenging.
I wouldn't have missed it even if I had a choice.
I thank you both for that life experience.
I close with this wish for you:
That you have long, healthy, interesting,
and challenging lives filled with the love
that only parents, spouses, children, grandchildren,
and close friends can bring into your life.

Mom

As you lay there in the hospital bed,
you seemed to be at rest
but unconscious of my presence.
I started to cry for you,
but I also knew that wouldn't help.
You were just ready to go
so that you could finally rest.
I just hoped that your pain was gone.
I believe that you are waiting for me
where we can be together again..

For David Matthew Munson

I can hardly believe it!
Time passes faster and faster as one ages.
You are now one year old,
and I have yet to hold my first great grandson
in my arms—although he is always
in my heart and as well as in my nightly prayers.
What do I ask of God for you
in those prayers?
*****

My petitions are identical
for all 12 of my grandchildren
and for my other two great grandchildren —
good health, mental, physical, and emotional,
a happy, fascinating, and demanding childhood,
totally encircled by the love of your parents,
sister, grandparents. relatives, and friends,.
I also ask for multiple opportunities for you
to develop. expand, and polish
your God-given gifts —
the talents, skills, abilities, and capacities
that will enable you to be
whatever you want to be —
and to do what you truly want to do
with your life—
so long as those wishes
are consistent with the laws
of both man and God.
*****

I close with this Gaelic blessing:
Dearest Father in Heaven,
bless David Matthew
and bless this day

-52

of his second year beginnings.
Smile upon David Matthew
and surround him, Lord,
with the soft mantle of Your love.
Teach David Matthew to follow
in Your footsteps and to live life
in the ways of love,
faith, hope, and charity.

For My Daughters 2

You deserve all the love I have for you
so never allow yourselves
to be heartbroken or sad.
Love is something that is meant to be
between daughters and their dad—
and it is a emotion that is supposed
to make you feel glad.

From the days of your births
I have always loved you with all my heart.
I can only hope that you always knew
that the love I have within my heart
is not for just one but for the two of you.

Too many people believe
that there is not enough love
for a parent to share with
more than one child.
I know that is dead wrong
because I have experienced love
for six kids,
and four of them are guys
rather than girls.

For James

Reserved, even taciturn, in speech and manner,
James is brilliant, clever, and gifted —
as attested in part by his three degrees:
B.S. in Psychology, M.S. in Information
Technology, and MBA, all awarded by
the Southern New Hampshire University.
Surviving a very difficult childhood and adolescence
following the untimely death of his mother
and his father's absence from his life,
James was reared by his grandmother.
He developed highly marketable skills:
accomplished computer expert,
manager of technical operations at UPS
and a tireless and expert entrepreneur —
purchasing and developing real estate,
a limousine service for Southern New Hampshire
and other business enterprises.
He is relentlessly on track to become
a very wealthy man — even a millionaire!
And, as of this writing, his net worth
undoubtedly exceeds that astounding amount.
Obvious to observers are James' pride and joy
is his beautiful and exceptionally bright and talented
6-year old daughter, Kaila. my great granddaughter.
He wants and demands only the very best for her
in terms of upbringing, education,
and abundant opportunities to grow and develop
into the lovely and talented woman
she is destined to become.

For Kaila on Her 6th Birthday

It was great seeing you a few weeks ago.
And I hope to see you here on Cape Cod soon.
I find it difficult to believe
that so many years have passed —
and that you are now six years old —
a very bright, lovely, and loving young lady!

Here are my feelings
In Haiku, Japanese verse
On your special day

My first great grandchild
A great gift in a long life
One to be treasured

Three essential traits
For success in any field
Smarts, grace, and wisdom

A good Mom is worth
More than one hundred teachers
In a youngster's life

Take care of yourself
Enjoy healthful food and drink
To live a long life

What I wish for you
My beautiful Kaila Lee
The best life offers.

HAPPY BIRTHDAY1

For Laine on Her 27th Birthday

Born on a Sunday and sharing her birthday,
not only with Space Shuttle Discovery 3's
return to earth, but also with
a huge number of noted artists, including
Lewis Carroll, author of *Alice in Wonderland,*
Wolfgang Armadeus Mozart, composer of *Figaro,*
Mikhail Baryshnikov, ballet superstar.
Donna Reed, actress, *From Here to Eternity*
Skitch Henderson, bandleader, *Tonight Show*
Jerome Kern, composer of *Showboat.*
But, of far greater importance,
Laine is my fifth grandchild, one of 12,
and the one with whom I have spent the most time
both at the Cape and in Rome, New York.
And that is only one of the reasons that:
she will always be special, she will always be loved
for the kindhearted way that she lives,
and she will always be wished joyful days in return
for the warmhearted gladness that she gives.
So, tonight and every night, my by-name prayers for Laine
always include petitions to The Blessed Mother,
my namesake intercessors, Saints William,
Raymond, and Francis,
and my patron, Saint Jude Thaddeus.
Those prayers request for Laine and those she loves,
long, healthy, productive, and rewarding lives—
and a loving and devoted spouse and caring children
to fulfill her dreams.

HAPPY BIRTHDAY!

For Leah on Her Birthday

Born on a Friday in a Leap Year,
she is a woman to be esteemed and treasured.
But, also of great importance, Leah arrived
during the Bicentennial of the United States,
the 200th anniversary of the signing
of the Declaration of Independence,
celebrated by parades, fireworks,
concerts, and other festivities across the country.
At that time, on average, a new house sold for $43,000,
monthly rentals went for $220, and
a gallon of gasoline cost only 59 cents.
Today, however, I'm grateful
for the pride Leah has brought to me
during the last few years,
for the strengths with which she has been blessed,
and the gifts she has brought to the Tracey family:
being an exemplary wife to Sean,
a loving daughter-in-law to my daughter, Kathy,
a congenial niece–in-law to my children,
Bill, Kevin, Brian, Maura, and Sean,
and an amiable cousin-in-law to my grandchildren.
I now look to the future with high hopes and dreams
for you and Sean, as well as for all of the members
of the Brandon and Tracey families.
Know too that you are cherished, appreciated,
and loved by your grandfather-in-law
and wished, not only a happy birthday,
but also a long life filled with love and happiness.

HAPPY BIRTHDAY!

For Sean T. on His 52ⁿᵈ Birthday

Born on a Friday in a Leap Year
and sharing his birthday,
with a large number of noted artists, including
Lewis Carroll, author of *Alice in Wonderland,*
Wolfgang Armadeus Mozart, composer of *Figaro,*
Mikhail Baryshnikov, ballet superstar,
Skitch Henderson, bandleader, *Tonight Show,*
and Jerome Kern, composer of *Showboat.*
But, of far greater importance,
arriving during the year that JFK was elected President,
Steve Jobs unveiled the Apple tablet PC iPad,
Elvis Pressley recorded *"Are You Lonesome Tonight?"*
and Soviet Premier Nikita Khrushchev
pounded his shoe on a desk
at the UN General Assembly in New York.
Today, however, I'm grateful
for the pride you've brought to me through the years
and for the strengths with which you have been blessed
from the beginning — academically, musically, socially,
and in leadership situations —
and more recently as an exemplary husband and father,
an exceptionally creative media producer-director,
a consummate marketer, and an accomplished
and highly successful businessman.
The latter are the talents and strengths you
had from the very beginning —
and I didn't know about until time and opportunities
made them clear to everyone.
I now look to the future with high hopes and dreams
for you, Lina, Victor, and Siara,
as well as for your brothers and sisters,
your nieces and nephews,

and your grand nieces and nephew.
So for all those times, situations, events,
and so many other things,
know that you are cherished, appreciated, and wished,
not only a happy birthday,
but also a long life filled with love and happiness.
HAPPY BIRTHDAY!

My Foster Mom

Sixty-five years ago, you passed away
Six and one-half decades ago, I cried all day.
I never got to say goodbye,
the stroke took you so quickly
that there was no time
to hold you hand and thank you
for your love and care
— and to hug you close.
But that's not what I miss the most.
I miss the most your caring face —
and the fact that no one can ever take your place.
My love for you in my heart will be,
until one day your smile I'll see.
I'll then be as happy as I can be
to see the mother I loved so very much,
but was never able to tell her such.
Your love for me I have known since small,
your hugs and kisses,
I treasure them all.
So wherever you are,
enjoy with me this out of the ordinary day,
just foster mother and foster son
in our own special way.

For Maura on Her 58th Birthday

You start another year
of your new life with Steve.
I trust and hope that it will be
even better than 2011+ part of 2012—
and that year plus has been very good!
The work that you have put into
your relationship
and your lovely little house
have been labors of love
for both Steve and you.
The patio and garden outside,
as well as the interior renovations
I have seen in photos,
provide evidence of your labor
and the livability of the product
of that effort.
My wishes and prayers for you and Steve
are that you will live the rest
of your lives in harmony and with
dedication and love —
instead of the discord, dissention,
and strife that marked and blemished
the years of your earlier marriages.
What I wish for you,
lovers Stephen and Maura,
is the best life gives.
I close with this Irish Blessing:
May your thoughts be as glad as the shamrocks.
May your hearts be as light as a song.
May each day bring you bright happy hours,
That stay with you all year long.

For Tamra on Her 37th Birthday

Born on a Wednesday and sharing her birthday,
with celebrities Adelina Patti, renowned operatic soprano,
Merle Oberon, celebrated actress, and Stan Kenton,
well-known jazz musician.
But, of far greater importance, she arrived
during the year declared by the United Nations
as the International Women's Year,
"Saturday Night Live" debuted on NBC,
the song of the year was *"The Way We Were,"*
and the Eagles' recordings of *"Best of My Love"*
and Elton John 's *"Island Girl,"* and
"July in the Sky with Diamonds" were released.
It was also the year that *"Wheel of Fortune"*
premiered on NBC, Elizabeth Seton was canonized,
to become the first American Roman Catholic saint —
and a gallon of gas cost 44 cents, and on average,
a new car cost $4,200, and a new home sold for $39.3 K,
Today, however, I'm grateful
for the pride you've brought to me through the years
and for the strengths with which you have been blessed
from the beginning — academically, musically,
and in leadership situations —
and more recently as an exemplary mother,
an accomplished financial advisor,
and a highly successful businesswoman.
I now look to the future with high hopes and dreams
for you, Kaila, and James, as well as for your aunts and uncles,
brothers and sisters, and your nieces and nephews,
.So for all those times, situations, and events,
know that you are cherished, appreciated, and wished,
not only a happy birthday,
but also a long life filled with love and happiness.

For Steve on His 54th Birthday

Yes, you're growing older,
but, that only means your getting better
— because you've learned more
about people, adversity, life,
and, most important, yourself.
And you have profited from your experiences.
Do you know that you share a birthday
with some very famous people?
To name just a few:
Composer Johannes Brahms,
actor Gary Cooper, and
football QB star Johnny Unitas.
And you missed by just one day,
May 6, film star Rudolph Valentino,
baseball star Willie Mays,
British PM Tony Blair,
and actor George Clooney.
In addition, some very important events
occurred on your birthday in 1958:
NASA was formed.
Sir Edmund Hillary reached the South Pole,
Elvis Presley was inducted into the U.S. Army,
and Charles DeGaulle became PM of France.
The most popular TV shows were
"Gunsmoke, " "Wagon Train, " "The Rifleman, "
and *"The Danny Thomas Show."*
Popular songs included
"At the Hop" by Danny and the Juniors,
"Twilight Time" by The Platters,
"All I Have to Do is Dream" by the Everly Brothers,
and *"Hard Headed Woman"* by Elvis Presley.
But, I have detoured too far from the main purpose

of this missive —
to laud your superlative personal qualities,
your various and diverse skills.
and the need for your family, friends,
workplace associates, and acquaintances
to value and salute you.
Perhaps that is best done
By a maxim followed by an Irish prayer.
*****

A good friend
is like a four leaf clover —
hard to find
and lucky to have.
Most of mine have gone to rest.
So I truly value the new one I have left.
*****

May your thoughts be as glad
as the shamrocks.
May your heart be as light
as a song.
May each day bring you
bright happy hours,
that stay with you
all the yearlong.

Haiku

If something goes wrong
Stay strong and keep unruffled
Show your composure

Hit it where they ain't
That's the goal of the batter
And the way to win

For Joanne on Her 63rd Birthday

What can I say to you
on this auspicious anniversary
—that I haven't said before?
Unless I engage in some obscenities
vulgarities, raunchiness, or shameless
language or expressions,
which I am loath to do —
not because they are unacceptable,
horrendous, or intolerable,
rather because using them is truly
out of character for me.
So, let me turn to the only alternative
available to me—
to tell you what you truly are
and what you mean to me.
You are invariably warm and loving,
not just with your immediate family
— although that is patently obvious
for anyone who observes you
with Brian, Jackie,
Mikie, Grace, or David—
but also with other members
of your extended family
as well as your many close friends.
You are fun-loving and funny!
Unlike most of us,
you are never downbeat,
gloomy, dejected, dispirited,
mopey, or morose.
And, most important to me,
you enjoy my cooking
— particularly my baked stuffed scallops,

as well as my company.
It's too bad that
we have seen each other so infrequently,
—less than a dozen times,
since you moved to Seattle —
twice on visits with my wife Kathleen,
two visits with Else-Marie
to attend Jackie's and Mikie's weddings.
and a handful of visits when you came
to weddings and visits with your brothers
and traveled to the Cape.
So, Joanne, this is for the times
we shared together,
Here's my prayer to St. Patrick:
as he brought new faith to Ireland,
so may he bring to you,
a touch of Irish happiness
in everything you do.
And, like the good Saint Patrick,
may your family, home, and life be blessed
with all God's special favors
that make you happiest.

Haiku

If you can't be good
Always be dependable
And you'll be valued

A prayer for you:
A long, hale, and happy life
Truly lacking strife

Four Brothers

The Tracey brothers,
four in number.
The middle two are twins,
the other two are older and younger.
One goes one way
and the three remaining
go in quite different directions.
Even the identical twins.
are as dissimilar in their lifestyles
as in their choices of women
and their record of marriages—
one is one for five
and the other is one for one.
Although as musicians
they played in the same show band,
only one of them performs
as a musician, if only rarely.
They never will be four again.
However, they still work together,
play together, and share holidays
and family events with each other.
It is obvious to even casual observers
that they truly love each other.
That is a source of pleasure and gratitude
for their nonagenarian father
— and their mother in Heaven.

A Kiss

Ecstasy for youth
Persecution for a child
Homage for the old

Friendship

Don't spar with your friend
It's better to be yielding
Than to be correct

Honoré L. Camiré

Henry was my friend for 68 years
and my across-the-street neighbor
with his wife Bernadette for 22 of those years.
I am the godfather of his youngest son,
William Raymond, and he is the godfather
of my youngest son, Sean Michael.
I first met Henry when I visited him in the hospital
where he was recovering from a serious accident.
Following graduation from High School in 1940,
we were employed for a short time
at the Whitney Reed Company, a toy-making shop.
During those years we frequently double-dated
for trips to Big-Band dances at the Totem Pole,
Kimball's Starlight, Canobie Lake, and Whalom Park.
We also served as each other's best man
at our weddings in July 1944 and November 1946.
After I entered college, Henry worked for 38 years
as a sales representative for the Prime Tobacco Company,
where he was well-known and highly respected
by clients in North Central Massachusetts.
Henry and Bernadette had five sons,
Andre, Paul, Robert, Thomas, and William,
four grandsons, and three great granddaughters.
Henry was a long-time member
of the Knights of Columbus, Leominster Lodge of Elks,
and Teamster's Local Union 170.
The Camires and Traceys were regular and frequent
participants in family get-togethers, weddings,
anniversaries, and holiday celebrations.
in Leominster, Ashby, Townsend,
Fitchburg, and Cape Cod.
My closest friend, Henry, died at age 83 March 1, 2006.

For Lucille On Her Birthday

Although I don't have the writing skills
that until recently I owned,
I would be remiss if I failed to memorialize
your birthday in verse.
So, herewith is my best effort to do so.
*****

I can hardly believe it!
And I'm betting that you feel the same.
Time passes faster and faster as one ages.
Although I don't know the exact year of your birth,
I'm sure that it is within a year or two of mine.
Despite the years that we have not been in touch,
you have often been in my thoughts
as well as in my nightly prayers.
What do I ask of God for you
in those prayers?
*****

My petitions are identical
for my closest friends,
all 12 of my grandchildren,
three great grandchildren, and their families:
good health, mental, physical, and emotional,
happy, interesting, and rewarding years,
totally encircled by the love of their children,
relatives. and friends.
I also ask for multiple opportunities for them
to use their God-given gifts —
whether they be cooking and baking,
knitting and seamstress skills,
or other talents, abilities, and capacities
that will enable them to be happy and productive.
*****

May joyfulness and peace touch your life
as consistently as your friendship has touched mine.
May the Year 2012
bring you good fortune,
good health, and every happiness.

For Jackie Livermore

Some people do not believe in the hereafter or angels.
Many of us still do and communicate often
with those we love who have passed to the other side.
You and your Mom
join me in that belief, that enduring faith.
So, you are a woman with attributes
that are distinctive, if not rare.
with a personality that makes you appealing
and a demeanor that is typically welcoming.
You are a goddaughter admired
and esteemed by her godfather —
and cherished and watched over from above
by Kay, your godmother and guardian angel.
So, Jackie, this is your day.
Enjoy it to the fullest.
You deserve the very best!
Kay is watching. She knows this truth:
You're someone who brings happiness
to everyone you know,
the world becomes a better place
wherever you go.
You're like a ray of sunshine
that gives life a warmer touch.
And that's the special reason,
you're admired and loved so much!
HAPPY BIRTHDAY!

Philip A. McMurray

I met Phil in September 1947,
when I was appointed temporary assistant professor
of education at Fitchburg State Teachers College.
A new colleague, Gertrude Cunningham,
asked me to pick up a faculty member
who needed a daily ride to the college.
I agreed and that started a friendship
that lasted until about 1977 when Phil retired.
In the intervening years Phil had been promoted
to chair of the English department, Dean of Men,
and Director of the Evening Division.
Phil was an Army veteran of the Pacific War.
He and his wife Margaret had twin daughters
while Kathleen was pregnant with Kevin and Brian,
who were born October 25 1948.
By that time we had both moved
into the Veterans' Project in South Fitchburg,
where I continued to drive Phil to the college
until several years later when we both moved to Ashby.
Finally, Phil purchased a car and drove himself.
When I moved on to the Army Security Agency,
I had received my doctorate from Boston University,
Phil had abandoned his pursuit of a doctoral degree,
and hired me as an evening division adjunct professor.
But our close friendship continued
with frequent visits to each other's homes —
and our families grew — mine to six and Phil's to 10 children.
Unfortunately, Phil lost four of his children — son Bernard,
and daughters Barbara, Janet, and Margaret (to breast cancer).
At the time of his death November 21, 1998,
Phil was survived by three sons, Philip Jr., Peter, and Michael,
and three daughters, Kathleen, Patricia, and Joan.

For Clarence on His 42nd Birthday

You start another year today,
and it is an auspicious and consequential one
because it includes your wedding day.
So let me begin by wishing you
and Stacey a happy, healthy, loving,
and long life together.
I know that your Mom, Else-Marie,
and your Daughter, Kiana,
love you unconditionally
and share your joy and happiness
— and you deserve that support
and approbation completely.
You have demonstrated your love
for your mother by your bi-weekly
weekend visits with her.
Similarly, you have shown your deep love
for your daughter
by your unfailing support, both financially
and emotionally, the weekends
and school vacations spent with her,
attendance at events of importance to her,
and unfailing attention
to her needs and wants.
So, in my eyes, as well as those
of your mother and daughter,
you are THE MAN!
I leave you with these Irish
blessings— one light-hearted
and the other very serious:
As you slide down the banister of life,
may the splinters never point the wrong way.
May you and Stacey see all your dreams come true.

Dr. C.L. John Legere

I hired Jack as a supervisor of student teachers
when I was director of training
at Fitchburg State Teachers College
and again when I was educational consultant
to the commandant of the US Army Security Agency
Training Center & School at Fort Devens.
Our wives and we were close friends for many years.
Jean (Bishop) Legere was a nursing student
at Burbank Hospital and Fitchburg State
before she and Jack were married.
Jack was the most creative, innovative,
and inspiring teacher I have ever known.
He, Dr. Ed Flynn, and I developed
the Systems Approach to Training,
which was adopted by all US military services
and scores of industrial corporation in the US.
Jack died at age 70 on February 5, 2000,
leaving his wife, three sons, two daughters,
10 grandchildren, and three great grandchildren.
He is greatly missed by everyone who knew him.

To Janice

Mother of my grandchildren, Kolby and Kaylyn.
May happiness always touch your life
as warmly as you have touched mine.
May the Year 2012 bring you good fortune,
good health, and every happiness.
I leave with this special Irish blessing:
May your blessings outnumber
the shamrocks that grow.
And may trouble avoid you wherever you go.

Ralph A. Curran

Born in New Ipswich, N.H. August 7, 1921,
Ralph moved to Ashby, graduating
from Ashby High School in 1939.
After working at Simons Saw and Steel as a heat treater,
he served with the 8th Army Air Force during World War II
and was in London during the Blitz.
He attended fighter pilot training in 1943,
married his wife Pauline O'Connor while on leave,
and attended the Vesper George School of Art,
intending to pursue a career as a commercial artist.
He attended Fitchburg State College
and, upon graduation,
replaced me as sixth grade teacher and principal
of the Dolly Whitney Adams school in Ashburnham. .
Soon thereafter, he was appointed
superintendent of schools,
the youngest school superintendent in Massachusetts.
Serving for ten years,
he reassumed the title of principal
when Ashburnham regionalized its school system
with Winchendon in 1959.
He retired in 1983 to his home
on Wyman's Lake and pursued his hobbies
of gardening and home remodeling.
Ralph was a very talented artist and craftsman.
He was a life-long member of the Holmes-Curran-Bennett
American Legion Post in Ashby
and the Massachusetts Teachers Association.
Ralph died at age 84, July 15, 2006,
leaving two sons, John and Thomas,
one daughter, Kathlyn, and three grandchildren.

Sweet Sue

I know you as
A woman with attributes that are unique
A personality that makes you appealing
A demeanor that makes you welcome
Professionalism that makes you a dedicated teacher.
And, in addition,
A cat lover par extraordinaire
A successful gardener and avid dahlia aficionado
An enthusiastic reader, concertgoer, and traveler,
And a skilled and accomplished knitter.

I regret that my family and I have not been
a continuing part of your life for so many years
Herewith you will know what kind of poem
I have (belatedly) written for you.
You are absolutely correct —
I cared for you from day one—
and have never stopped caring for you.
I was devastated when you and Kevin divorced,
and I never understood why that happened.

You have always been on my mind
and in my heart.
Since your and Kevin's wedding day,
you have always been and will always be
Sweet Sue, my very first daughter-in-law —
rightfully and emotionally
even though such a designation is not
in harmony with established canons,
laws, edicts, or social conventions.
I couldn't care less.
That's just how I feel about you.

Know too that I am truly elated
that you and Dennis found each other
and have enjoyed a long and loving marriage.

He is a talented, engaging, accomplished,
good, caring, and gentle man—
one of a very rare kind,

Here are my prayers, hopes, and wishes
for you and Dennis.
I wish and pray for continued good health,
happiness, and adventure for both of you.

I sum up with modified lyrics of the Bing Crosby
version of the popular song, "Sweet Sue":

Every star above, knows the one I love
My daughter-in-law, Sweet Sue —just you
And the moon on high, knows the reason why_
Sweet Sue - is you!

Someone else it seems, didn't share my dreams
About a lifetime of being close to you_
Without knowing that you'd be all right
I didn't know what I'd do.

That everything turned out fine was a wonderful find.
So, in this heart of mine, you still live all the time
Ooh, Sue – yes, it's you

Haiku

Lighten up today
Give yourself a holiday
You deserve one now

An old-fashioned skill
Graceful cursive penmanship
Displaced by texting

The Women in My Life

After *Strands of Memory Reprised* was published in 2011,
I discovered that I had seriously under-reported
the number and identities of the women
who played important roles in my life.
Here follows an attempt to correct that mistake.

I'm a very lucky man. I have had two mothers,
Pauline Eva, my birth mother, and her sister, Josephine Mary,
who nurtured me and brought me to adulthood
after my mother died in childbirth.
In addition to my two daughters,
Katheen and Maura,
I have eight granddaughters,
Tamra, Jackie, Mikie, Laine,
Katie, Kolby, Kaylyn, and Siara,
and two great granddaughters, Kaila and Grace.
My wife, Kathleen, my Dad's second wife,
Sarah McNamara O'Neill.
my sisters, Mary Kirby and her daughter, Patricia; Pauline
Kidik and her daughter Barbara, Margaret DiPietrantonio
and her daughter Elizabeth, and Eileen Hendershaw;
my sisters-in-law Terri O'Neill and daughter Christine,
Margaret O'Neill and daughters Kathy Bartos and
granddaughters Deborah and Sandra; Karen Sinclaire and
granddaughters, Kristin and Kelli; Sandra O'Neill and
daughters, Elizabeth, Mary, and Jean; Martha Boucher and
daughters, Maureen and granddaughter Brooke, and Karen;
my grandmothers, Minnie Burgoyne, Mary Kileen Tracey,
and Anne O'Neill, my mother-in-law Lillian Doheny,
my O'Neill aunts, Mary, Christine, and Rebecca;
my Burgoyne aunts, Minnie, Margaret, Aleda, Laura, Eva,
Elsie (my god mother), and Clara; my Tracey aunts, Margaret,

Elizabeth, Nellie, Delia, and Maime;
My cousins Ruth, Mary, and Alice Burgoyne,
my grandmothers-in-law, Ida (Aiti) Ahola
and Hannah Doheny; the Doheny aunts,
Mary, Anna, and Helen; the Ahola aunts, Maime, Louella,
and Margareeta, are all members of my extended famly
and many are now in Heaven,
Fortunately, I now have Else-Marie, my lifeline
and friend forever.
I also have two goddaughters, Jackie and Christine,
and her daughters, Sarah and Carolina;
four daughters-in-law. Joanne, Lina, Lin Li, and Suzanne;
one grand daughter-in-law, Leah,
and six ex-daughters-in-law,
Susan, Janet, Kimberly, Janice, Kathy, and Linda.
And there were dozens of first cousins,
some of whom I have never even met.
The ones I remember best are Anne, Ruth, Alice, Mary,
Catherine, and Claire Burgoyne, Jerri Cox, and Betty.DeWitt.
Of course there were some girl friends —
Mary Shaunessy, Kathleen Smithhammer, Eleanor Bird,
Theresa Gerante, Mary Hanley, Janet Kolazik, Jane Patak,
Jeanne Fournier, Lucille Belleveau, and many other feminine
friends of all ages: Doris, Norma, Mary, Janet, Jane, Jean,
Bernadette, Lucille, Kathleen D, Helen-Lou, Kathleen H,
Amy Beth, Jeanne, Martha, Annabel, Elizabeth, Ellen,
Susan, Libby, Alicia, Morgan, Peggy,
Margaret, Stephanie, Judith, Mary, Marguerite,
Marge, Sheila, Marti, Irene, Marie,
and other long-ago, long-time friends,
I cannot omit mention of special teachers,
Sister Mary Austin 5th grade, St. Leo's School, Miss McCarty,
Professor of Speech, FSTC, Mrs. Manning Morrill. teacher of
English, Senior Year at LHS, Helen Curry, Professor of Music,

FSTC, Marie Gearan, Director of Training, FSTC
and Professor, Boston College
and my professional associates,
AMACOM book editor Adrienne Hickey,
Gertrude Cunningham, Supervisor of Student Teaching,
Rachel Bruce, Assistant Director of Training. Catherine
Weston, Lillian Tater, Belle Nixon, Florence Conlon, Professor
of Art FSTC, Signe Atilla,
Captain Mary Barker, and Major Judy Jackson,
And then there were my administrative assistants,
sequentially over a 25-year period,.
Irene Jacobowski, Nina, Myra Hansberry,
Marie Hanley, Ruth Dufresne, and Sofia Charron,
All of these women have touched my life in significant ways.
They have made me more sensitive,
more caring, more loving,
as well as more effective and productive
as a person, husband, father, grandfather,
teacher, manager, and friend.
They have given me far more than I have given them.
I shall be eternally grateful for their affection, understanding,
and helpfulness, thoughtfulness, support.
—and love!

Haiku

Be a rising star
That dream is never too big
Put fear behind you

Don't be judgmental
Always be willing to help
Keep an open mind

Dr. Edward B. Flynn, Jr.

Ed was a student of mine when I was a
professor of education and director of training
at Fitchburg State Teachers College.
He served in the US Army during the Korean War.
I hired him as a supervisor of student teaching.
Shortly after I was employed
at Fort Devens as educational consultant,
I recruited Ed as an education specialist in evaluation.
He completed a doctorate in educational psychology
at the University of Oklahoma while on leave from FSTC.
Promoted to the position of director of evaluation,
Ed earned outstanding performance ratings
as he did in every position that he ever held.
He collaborated with Dr. Jack Legere and me
in developing the Systems Approach to Training
adopted by the US Armed Forces
and many corporate training departments.
Ed was a talented teacher and effective administrator.
He and his wife Helen became our close friends.
They parented two sons and two daughters,
Ed died at age 67 October 13, 1997.

Haiku

Be adventurous
Try new things at least one time
You'll be glad you did

Days are all too short
Enjoy the small things in life
Love yourself today

Thomas B. Doheny, Jr.

Tommy was not only my brother-in-law,
he was my supporter and very best friend.
Redheaded Tommy was born in Fitchburg,
February 28, 1925, brother of my wife, Kathleen,
and his younger siblings, Jackie, and Martha.
Tommy was an irrepressible, fun-loving,
outspoken, bold, and loyal guy.
He was fun to be with, and we spent hours together
philosophizing about life—
of course when he was not engaged
in playing practical jokes on his parents,
other relatives, friends, and me.
After graduating from St. Bernard's High School,
Tommy enlisted in the Navy in December 1942
and graduated in April 1943
from the Naval Hospital School, Camp LeJeune, NC.
He was assigned to the Marine Corps
as a combat medic.
When Kathleen and I were having trouble with
her relatives, mainly her Aunt Mary,
Tommy supported us from overseas.
In a letter to Kathleen, October 22, 1943,
he wrote, "I'm advising you and Bill
to get married as soon as you possibly can.
Never mind what anyone says, Kay.
Use your own judgment. I know that you have
a good head on those shoulders."
Tommy was killed in action September 15, 1944,
He was a real hero, a combat medic,
during the invasion of Peleliu in World War II
while serving as a Pharmacist's Mate Third Class
with the U.S. Marine Corps.

WAR

Most were just young kids
Who had seen little of life
But were shown hades

The Last Reunion

It was emotionally draining but also heart-warming
to meet fellow members of the LST Association in Missouri.
At a conference room in the hosting hotel,
I looked around the room at sailor veterans in their 80s,
many with their wives of 40 or more years,
and listened entranced as they described their adventures
while island-hopping during the Pacific War at sea —
as seen through the aging eyes of men
of the amphibious World War II Navy.
They were all LST veterans,
crewmen and officers of the 328-foot landing ships
that carried tanks, trucks, supplies,
and Army and Marine troops —
and, in the case of my LST 117,
four physicians and several enlisted medics
to handle casualties (as an auxiliary hospital ship).
These amphibious ships landed their cargo on beaches,
braving intense artillery, mortar, and sniper fire,
Kamikaze aircraft, and suicide swimmer attacks.
LSTs participated in the Pacific War invasions of Guam,
the Solomons, the Carolines, the Philippines, Iwo Jima,
Okinawa, and other islands, and finally occupied Japan.
With well-deserved pride in their voices,
they described how they took their chances
and fought their war with courage and competence,
laughing and crying, eyes flowing with tears —
recalling and saddened that many of their comrades died,
while others lived to swap stories over the intervening years.
These brave men were the combat-seasoned sailors of the LST
Amphibious Navy, proud that they had served their country,
and now they were not at sea,
but celebrating their survival in Branson, Missouri!

My Longest Day
October 20, 1944

Navigating the Western Pacific aboard the LST 117
on the way to the invasion of the Philippine Islands,
the next "stepping stone" to the Japanese homeland.
Standing watch as officer of the Deck (OOD)
on the flying bridge high above the ship's main deck.
Numbering a total of twelve 328-foot LSTs,
the convoy also included six heavily loaded
with about two hundred soldiers,
six General Sherman Tanks,
several 2X2 Army trucks, and two pontoons,
accompanied by four Landing Ships Infantry (LCIs)
one Landing Ship Medium (LSM).
one Landing Ship Dock (LSD),
and, for air assault protection, two destroyers (DDs).

Worrying about the next day and how I would respond
to combat action involving live fire
by Japanese artillery, mortars, rifles, and grenades,
Kamikazes, and suicide swimmers.
Hoping that I would perform professionally,
courageously, and in accordance with Navy traditions.
Completing my watch with difficulty keeping on station
due to bad weather, lack of radar, and zigzagging
in submarine evasive maneuvers.

Being relieved at 0000 (midnight) by Ensign Barney Moses,
I repaired to my bunk for much needed sleep.
Rudely awakening at 0300 by the ship's earsplitting klaxon
sounding Battle Stations, I quickly dressed in my fatigues.
Donning my web belt, a holstered 45-caliber Colt pistol,
ammunition, a sheathed combat knife,

a small first aid kit— and my jungle green steel helmet
decorated with "Tracey" in red paint on its front.

Moving quickly to my battle station on the forecastle,
centered between two 40-mm antiaircraft gun tubs,
each weapon served by an ammo loader and two gun trainers,
one for horizontal bearing and the other for azimuth tracking.
Checking the harnesses of the sailors
manning the eight 20-mm antiaircraft weapons
and the 12 sailors firing the 50-caliber machines guns.
Dropping the stern anchor as the ship approached
the beach of Leyte Island,
to assist in withdrawing the ship after unloading.

Enduring the pandemonium caused by the bombardment
by battleships, cruisers, and destroyers
offshore behind us softening up the Japanese defenders
by using 16-, 14-, 12-, and 8-inch shells.
Braving the deafening sound of 16-inch rounds overhead
on their way to their targets whooshing
like speeding express trains.
Adding to the clamor were our own AA weapons
when they began firing at Kamikazes
and mortar fire coming from the Japanese on the island aimed
at the beached LSTs.

Feeling like I was inside a bass drum,
with the deck plates vibrating from both the incoming rounds
and the outgoing projectiles.
Enduring the bedlam for what seemed like an eternity,
my attention was drawn to a very young crewman,
sitting on the deck, knees drawn up,
and his hands covering his face

as he cried, completely terrorized.
Trying to calm him, I shouted at him to move to some cover
provided by the entrance to the port side tank deck ladder.
He seemed to be getting his fear under control and complied.

Seeing the chaplain making his rounds
and attempting to comfort and encourage the sailors.
Watching him felled by what later was found to be
a piece of shrapnel embedded in his buttocks
after the medics carried him to the surgery below decks.
Suddenly, I was knocked to the deck by a blow
to the front of my helmet.
Picking myself up, although somewhat dazed,
I learned that it was a shell fragment that had hit me.
Discovering that my helmet that had saved me
from a severe head wound.
although the piece badly dented my pot helmet.

The Chaplain was the only LST 117 crew member
to receive the Purple Heart on that invasion.
Serving my four-hour watch that night,
while the ship was still beached,
high above the deck on the flying con,
with star shells lighting up the sky—
I was an easy target for Japanese snipers and mortars.
Fortunately, I escaped injury despite the constant
whiz of bullets and the whoosh
of arriving mortars rounds. .

Retracting from the beach the next morning,
we later learned that the LST that took our beach slot
received direct hits, killing several crew members
and wounding many others.
Our ship was thereafter known as the Lucky Eleven-Seven.

That marked the end of my first day of combat
— the day that I qualified for award
of the Asiatic Pacific Campaign, Philippine Liberation,
Philippine Independence, and World War II Victory Medals
—and the Combat Action and Philippine Presidential Unit
Citation Ribbons.

The LST

On June 7, 2005, with my oldest son, Bill Jr.
and grandsons L.B. and Tim,
we climbed the gangplank of the restored WW II LST 325,
toured that ship from the tank deck to the bridge,
the gun tubs fore and aft, the wardroom and galley,
crew's quarters and my cabin in its sister ship, the LST 117.
The captain of the 325 also gave me permission
to climb to the flying bridge,
where I had served as OOD underway
during my 14-months aboard the LST 117.
As I began the long and arduous climb,
I soon realized that I was physically unable to make it
and had to abandon the attempt.
Despite that setback, I am glad that I had the experience—
as well as the thrill of watching the ship
pass through the Cape Cod Canal on its voyage to Boston.
Although not the handsomest ship that sailed the seas,
in value per ton, no other warship could match the LST.
A Navy ship does well what its designers planned,
when manned by an expert crew and competent command.
Since that's the metric applied to fighting ships at sea,
the highest regard and esteem must go to the LST—
a ship that brought men, weapons, and equipment to the fight
and from beaches carried the wounded to hospital ships,
their doctors, and nurses, for life-saving treatment.

Sergeant James E. O'Neill

Awaiting the completion of dental repairs
before he enlisted in the Army Air Corps
in the spring of 1942.
Being drafted and sent to Fort Devens
for Infantry Basic Training,
Receiving orders to Maxwell Field, AL
for pilot training prior to receipt of orders
to an infantry unit.
Enduring the rigorous physical and mental training
at the Army Air Corps' "West Point,"
including cadet hazing.
Graduating and being sent to primary pilot training
at Lodwick Academy in Avon Park, Fl.
"Washing out" due to air sickness and
and transferring to the Radio School in Sioux Falls, S.D.
Graduating as a Radio Operator and sent to Biggs
Field, deep in the heart of Texas,
for training as a radio operator and gunner
on the 10-man crew of a B-24 bomber.
At age 26. serving as the oldest member of the crew
(Pilot 22, Navigator 22, and Bombardier 21),
where he was called "Pop."
Becoming ineligible for continuing flight status
due to ear and sinus infections and headaches
caused by high altitude flights.
Transferring to Selfridge Field, MI
awaiting overseas assignment.
Departing Hampton Roads, VA on a Liberty ship,
European destination unknown.
Sleeping on the bulkhead of the weather deck
to avoid the over-crowded troop quarters below.
Enduring the cold, occasional rain storms,

and the zigzagging course of the ship
required to avoid attack by German submarines.
Making port, following a bad storm,
at Bari on the east coast of Italy.
Boarding the cattle car of an awaiting train,
40 men to a car.
Traversing Italy through Caserta
to cold, muddy, and badly war-damaged Naples.
Pitching tents in six inches of water and mud,
sans showers or a change of clothing
after more than three weeks of travel,
cold, exhausted, and stinking.
Flying out of Foggia Air Strip in a C-54
through Algeirs to Casablanca, Morocco.
Boarding another plane the next day,
flying on through the Western Sahara
and Mauritania to Dakar in Senegal.
Having changed into summer chinos,
taking the long haul from Dakar southeast
over the Ivory Coast and the Gold Coast (now Ghana)
near the Equator to Roberts Air Field, near Monrovia,
the capital of Liberia, home for over the next year.
Stepping out of the plane and walking into an oven —
the heat was fierce during the day (130F)
and the humidity always oppressive.
Losing more than 15 pounds in the first month.
and dropping more weight thereafter.
Assigned to the Army Air Corps Communications Service
as a radio operator working on the radio tower,
and handling radio traffic nightly
using voice and Morse code,
Receiving and returning transmissions to aircraft
coming across the Atlantic from Bogata, Columbia

or Ascension Island in the South Atlantic.
and directing them to and landing them
on Roberts Air Field (130 F).
In off duty time, befriending and assisting
a missionary Catholic priest, singing at the enlisted club
with a four-piece combo, transmitting recorded programs
from the United States, making newscasts at 1200 and 1800
for the local radio station, running the post theater,
and writing a weekly mimeographed newspaper.
Boarding a C-47 for transfer to a new station
on the Sahara at Villa Cisneros in Rio de Oro,
Spanish Morocco, an airstrip located on a peninsula
jutting into the Atlantic.
Living on a flat desert point of land with no vegetation,
manned by a lieutenant and ten enlisted men,
a strip built to serve as an emergency-landing place
for aircraft flying to Liberia from Europe.
Having only a small radio shack on the ground,
and lacking an air control tower, it was only equipped
with a tall antenna near the end of the runway.
The crew was responsible only for directing
and landing aircraft for refueling or emergencies.
Living in tents until Quonset huts were built,
lacking freshwater and using Lister bags
filled with treated water, or importing fresh water
from the Canary Islands — until successful
in digging through the sand and coral
to hit fresh water.
Handling an emergency during a Sgt. O'Neill watch.
Happening in the late afternoon, a blanket of fog
rolled in over the air strip, lowering the ceiling
to 100 feet or less.
Receiving a call from a transport plane carrying
a group of combat veterans on their way home

after surviving the War in Europe.
Recognizing a very bad situation
because the aircraft was just about out of fuel
and needed to land immediately.
Lacking the equipment required to land safely
under low visibility conditions, and needing help.
Having radio contact with the experienced pilot,
but dealing with the problem of avoiding the high antenna
at the end of the runway, and another tall tower
at a nearby Spanish installation —
and the lack of an experienced ground controller
in a well-equipped control tower to talk the plane down.
Sgt Jim O'Neill was on the hook,
and communicated that fact to the pilot.
Despite repeated and unsuccessful attempts
to correct the plane's landing flight path.
following "Get up! " and "Go around!" directions,
the tension became agonizing.
Struggling to control himself so as not to rattle the pilot,
Jim talked the pilot onto the right flight path,
avoid the towers, and make a safe landing—
minutes of suspense and awful pressure
for both Jim and the pilot.
Following the landing, the pilot found Jim, and said,
"Thank you! Without your help, we would never have made it."
Jim received a Letter of Commendation for his efforts
"in the spirit and actions of the Army Air Corps"
from the commanding officer of the AACCS.

Haiku

Vets of World War II
The Greatest Generation
A breed that's dying

Navy Java

Drinking coffee was not my habit before World War II.
Dunking doughnuts occasionally
in creamed and sugared coffee was my brew.
Changing my drinking habits occurred early
in my shipboard life aboard an LST,
while standing three 4-hour watches per day
in the Navy as an OOD.
The watches were lonely and long
and filled with anxiety and tension—
zigzagging to avoid Japanese submarines
and changing course and speed—
maneuvers that required one's undivided attention.
Caffeine available 24 hours per day in the ship's mess,
in the form of extra strong and black Navy Java,
provided the ultimate solution.
The brew was served in stained cups
by a seaman gofer assigned to that duty.
Invariably it was so strong that it could stand
without a mug — with just a spoon in your hand.
I always ordered the draft with a generous
measure of canned evaporated milk
to moderate the bitterness of the aged brew—
blithely disregarding the rumor
that the canned milk brought to the bridge
was unlikely to have ever been in a fridge.
And if it failed to pour or run,
it was probably a leftover from World War I.
Down in the engine room below,
the motor mech crew was rumored to favor an arcane brew.
As they carried out their mission-related crafts,
they used that concoction to grease the ship's shaft.

Nevertheless I continued to drink that Java,
over time diminishing the amount of canned milk,
and the addition of sugar,
until the brew was entirely strong and black.
When I returned to civilian life in 1946,
I was then totally hooked on caffeine.
I continued to drink at least six cups of strong coffee
every workday to reduce the pressures
and stress of a difficult position until I retired in 1982
and took a less-demanding and more pleasurable job.
Since then, I have been a tee-totaller
never again using that caffeinated concoction.
With a heart condition, I no longer
need it —nor can I tolerate it.
So another bad habit has been terminated.

Haiku

Youth of all races,
Sizes, genders, uniforms
Some became heroes

Large slow targets all
World War II LSTs
Amphibious ships

Vets of World War II
The Greatest Generation
A breed that's dying

Tommy Doheny
KIA at Peleliu
A real war hero.

Shipmates Forever

On that long final voyage
all of us are destined to make,
sailing toward a distant beach
the living have yet to take.

Knowing that we all must
follow the same compass course,
we offer those on that voyage,
the traditional seafarer's wish:
"Smooth sailing and following seas."
For those mariners, and we
fated to make the same voyage,
will be shipmates forever.
And that wish and prayer
includes my brother-in-law.
and closest friend.
Tommy, killed in action at Peliliu
in World War II,

Haiku
War is hell on earth
It destroys people and hope
It gives back nothing

The hallmarks of war
Bedlam, chaos, confusion
Fear and loneliness

Most were just young kids
Who had seen little of life
But were shown hades

Nature

A wonder to see
An osprey diving for fish
To attract his mate

The Northeaster of 2011

On October 28, 2011, Hurricane Irene,
although still packing a powerful punch,
was downgraded to a tropical storm.
However, it pummeled and battered Massachusetts
after roaring up the Eastern Seaboard,
dumping torrential rains
and sending rivers and streams over their banks,
pounding the shoreline with relentless waves,
and toppling trees and power lines.
But, that was just the beginning
of what turned into a very bad weekend,
nicknamed, Snowtober.
After Saturday and Sunday's onslaught,
October 29th and 30th,
many people endured up to a week,
and in some cases more days, without power—
cut off when trees, large branches,
and telephone poles crashed down
taking the wires with them.
Thousands of homes and businesses were affected.
Following the rare October storm,
they were without electricity and heat.
Amtrak cancelled train service on Monday
between Boston and Philadelphia, and **Acela Express**
discontinued service between Boston and Washington
due to flooding and debris on the tracks.
Many communities postponed or cancelled
"trick-or-treating" for youngsters because of
downed power lines and trees and limbs,
as well as dangerous walking and driving conditions.
It was a weekend to remember
along with a prayer that it not be repeated.

Dolphins

Aside from domestic pets, dolphins are the most loved
animals in the sea and everywhere else on earth.
Not only are they intelligent, but also highly social,
talented aquatic acrobats, with their own language.
And they also appear to have an affinity for humans.
On countless occasions over many years,
dolphins have come to the rescue
of people in distress or danger at sea.
The rash of dolphin strandings along Cape Cod Bay
during January and February 2012 was unusually large.
During that period, the International Fund for Animal Welfare,
augmented by staffers of other local
marine mammal protection groups and volunteers,
has responded to 129 strandings
between Dennis and Wellfleet, a 25-mile stretch of beach.
Only 37 were rescued, and the remaining 92
either died before they were helped
or were so near death that they were euthanized soon after.
Why do dolphins and other marine animals
strand and others do not?
Could climate change be a factor?
The shape of Cape Cod— a fishhook of land
formed by a glacier
that juts out into the Atlantic Ocean?
Tides and shore land geography?
Acoustic disruptions in the ocean caused by ships and sonar
or changes in the earth's magnetic field, solar storms,
geomagnetic activity, geologic or seismic disturbances?
Or could it be toxins from septic systems,
agricultural practices, industrial processes,
or other human-caused sources of pollutants?
We just don't know!

Some data have been collected since 1999:
location, date, and time, species, sex, and size,
necropsies that include blood analyses, and organ samples
inspected for disease and parasites.
So, the factors in dolphin strandings are complex
and have not been collected long enough
to know what's unusual.
The answers lie in more research.
We still have a lot to learn!

An Annual Risky Journey

Why does a female snapping turtle
cross a highway with heavy traffic?
Because she wants to get to the other side
where she has always laid her eggs.
Why does she lay her eggs?
Because of the instinct to propagate her species.
Why is she sometimes killed
when making that crossing?
Because she moves so slowly that speeding cars
and careless drivers are unable to avoid hitting her.
If she makes the crossing safely and buries her eggs,
where and how will they be incubated?
Where she buries them and by the warmth of the sun.
She will then have accomplished her mission
if she makes it safely back across the highway
and returns to the pond where she lives.
She will repeat that dangerous trip
the following year.
Such is the life of a snapping turtle
on Route 6 of Lower Cape Cod.

The Sea

I have always loved the sea—
just as much as my dad loved it.
He joined the Navy in 1906 and was assigned
to the battleship USS Rhode Island.
Between 16 December 1907 and 22 February 1909,
President Theodore Roosevelt sent the "Great White Fleet,"
consisting of 16 battleships and several destroyer escorts,
around the world to demonstrate America's sea power.
My Dad went with the fleet as an Electrician's Mate.
When I was a boy, Dad regaled me
with stories about his travels.
That is why I joined the Navy in 1942
and served in the Pacific War.
During my life I have traveled over and on oceans, seas,
and other large bodies of water.
In addition to the Pacific, South Pacific, Atlantic,
South Atlantic, and Indian oceans,
I have traversed the Philippine, China, South China,
Celebes, Coral, Bearing, and Caribbean Seas,
the Bay of Fundy, Lake Champlain, Sea of Japan,
Gulf of Mexico, Massachusetts and Cape Cod Bays, Nantucket
and Long Island Sounds,
and the North, Irish, Mediterranean,
Black. and Aegean Seas.
The sea is also the main reason we moved to Cape Cod
— to be near the sea. and its inviting beaches.
But, the people who live and work on Cape Cod
are inextricably intertwined with the sea.
Surrounded by salt water and dependent on the ocean
for their livelihoods, directly or indirectly.
Most have come because they love it here.
In some way they are inspired by the sea,

knowing it's close by, feeding from it,
moving around in it and over it,
walking, playing, and swimming in it or boating on it.
But, most of all, they are spiritually nourished by it.
They also write about the ocean, sing about it, photograph it,
find romance in its proximity, and share love,
both human and canine, along its beaches
during the spring, summer, and fall, even during the winter.
People prepare this special place and share the sea
with the rest of the world, coaxing visitors
to stay in our cottages, bed and baths, inns, and restaurants.
They also fall in love, marry, or honeymoon here
by the cobalt waters and crashing waves,
teach their children to build sandcastles,
ride waves, explore tide pools, swim and sail,
and learn to love the sea as much as their parents do.
Artists come to the cape to capture feelings and emotions
by painting, photographing, and writing about the sea
so that others can take home reminders
of their experiences when they must say adieu.
And let us not forget the animals
that are provided a home by the sea
—the bustling cities of life under its surface —
the fish and shellfish, the diving dolphins,
the ever-curious seals, and the breaching humpback,
right, and killer whales.
And above the oceans, the many species of birds,
from swooping gulls, to scuttling sandpipers
and piping plovers.
People come from near and far to see the many rare
and endangered birds
among the 12 million that in one night
have been spotted migrating over Cape Cod,
If we live like we love the ocean,

we would ban the plastic bags and balloons
that wind up in the ocean,
the poisons that are released into our estuaries and bays
by highway runoff, septic and wastewater systems,
and industrial-size windmills
and power plants that exploit and threaten the survival
of wildlife in, on, and above the sea.
Many of us have learned what the Wampanoag
have always known:
that the seas are sacred, that no one can own them,
that we cannot take more of the sea's resources
than we need to sustain ourselves,
and that everything we do has consequences
for generations to come.
Let us live like we love the ocean – because we do!
*****

Thank God, the Creator
For the vast playground
He has given us to enjoy,
Waves swishing on the beach
Music to my ears.
The seas talk to us
With sparkling waters,
the sea foam feathering the sandy shore.

We are tied to the ocean.
And when we go back to the sea,
whether it is to sail or to watch –
we are going back from whence we came.
— John F. Kenney

The Southern Cross

On many cloudless nights while on watch conning
the LST 117 as it island-hopped
underway to another invasion in the Pacific War.
I looked with wonder at the beautiful constellation,
The Southern Cross,
also known as the Crux Constellation,
Latin for cross.
It is the most commonly known
and easily identifiable
of all the southern constellations.
It can be viewed in the night sky
from most of the Southern hemisphere
near the horizon at practically anytime of the year
— and even from places
in tropical latitudes of the Northern hemisphere
for a few hours every night
during the northern winter and spring.
The four brightest stars in the constellation
form a cross pattern.
Sailors have relied on the Cruz
to help navigate their ships.
The Southern Cross is sometimes confused
with the nearby False Cross by stargazers.
Crux is somewhat kite-shaped,
and it has a fifth star (Crucis).
The False Cross is diamond shaped,
somewhat dimmer on average,
does not have a fifth star,
and lacks the two nearby "Pointer Stars."
The national flags of Australia and New Zealand
carry versions of the Southern Cross.

Shipboard Observations

Sunsets in the Pacific
The sunsets in the Pacific are the most beautiful
anywhere on earth except on Cape Cod.
As the sun dips below the horizon,
the sky changes from pink to deep red,
then to greens and purple.
Suddenly it is night,
and the stars in their constellations
shine brightly against a jet-black background.
The ship moves quietly through the dark waters
with only the faint hum of its diesels
reaching your ears.
*****

The Southern Hemisphere Phenomenon
In the Northern Hemisphere the water in a toilet bowl
circles counter-clockwise when you flush it.
Below the Equator, however,
the toilet water always circles clockwise.
On my first voyage below the Equator,
from Hawaii to New Guinea,
I noted that marvel
as I awaited the beginning of the infamous
initiation into the Ancient Order of the Deep,
transforming me from a Pollywog to a Shellback.
*****

Crossing the International Date Line
The first time I made the crossing
of the 180th Meridian, the IDL, on 9/20/1944.
I skipped 9/19/1944
because one loses a day when traveling West
and repeats one day when traveling East.

Mark Twain had this to say about the trip:
"We must lose a day out of our lives,
a day never to be found again.
We shall all die one day earlier
than from the beginning of time
we were ordained to die.
We shall be a day behind through all eternity."
*****

Ocean birds
Around and above the Pacific Ocean
there are many birds.
The most common of course are the sea gulls.
But there is a special variety of seagull—
the black-beaked Gooney Bird of Midway Island.
There is one legendary bird, however,
that you will probably never see.
Sailors claim that it inhabits the islands
surrounding New Guinea, or Papua as it is now called.
I spent a lot of time in New Guinea's harbors,
at Milne Bay and Manus Island.
but I never saw the famous Kiwi bird.
This famed bird is renowned
for its acrobatics.
It flies at a high rate of speed
in ever decreasing concentric circles,
until it flies up its own anus.

Haiku

Nature has gone wild:
Hurricanes. floods, tornadoes
Earthquakes and wildfires

Old Cliff

During the summer of 1040, I worked
on my grandfather Burgoyne's farm
with my blind Uncle Ed in Ellenburg, N.Y.
In addition to feeding the chickens, milking cows,
shoveling manure, and doing other odd jobs.
I worked in the fields haying—
mowing, raking, and bringing hay to the barn
in a wagon behind Old Cliff, a very old horse.
Of course I spent a lot of time
viewing Old Cliff's rear end.
Cliff had hemorrhoids, large ones!
When he passed gas, as he often did,
purple rosettes as big as a fist,
slowly blossomed out of his anus —
quickly followed by a strong and pungent odor.
which immediately reached my nose
only a very few feet away.
A few minutes later, the rosettes would recede
into his behind, armed and ready
for the next discharge of gas.

Milking the "Girls"

Grandpa had a herd of 24 Holstein milk cows.
One of my jobs, both morning and night,
was to milk six of the "girls."
Regularly at least three of the cows waited until
I was milking them to relieve themselves.
Either singly or in unison, they would raise their tails
and drop large flaps of manure
and/or liquid into the trough behind them—
for me to shovel out then or the next morning.

Orion, the Hunter

I have been a neophyte stargazer since 1938
when my high school science teacher
insisted that we learn to recognize
the most common constellations.
My favorite star group is Orion, the Hunter.
That giant constellation is visible
in the Northern Hemisphere
from late fall through the winter months.
Looking at the night sky on cold, clear
winter nights, you can't miss it.
And once you have seen the outline
of the hunter's body, you'll never forget it.
Named for the great hunter in Greek mythology,
Orion was mentioned twice even earlier
in the Book of Job in the Old Testament.
Orion's most prominent features are his belt,
three bright stars in a row.
Surrounding the belt are four bright stars
outlining the hunter's body,—the two top
ones are his shoulders, and the two lower ones
are his knees or thighs.
Hanging from his belt is an array
of three bright stars — his sword.
Not all three are true stars.
The middle one is actually a giant nebula,
a cloud of gas about 1,000 light years away.
At the time of this writing (early spring),
Orion is beginning to slip toward the eastern horizon
and will soon disappear into the sun.
Like all winter night stars, Orion's stars
shine all summer, but they are invisible in sunlight.
When Orion disappears, winter is really over.

The Pacific Typhoon

I served aboard the USS LST 117
during two typhoons.
One of them occurred on 18 December 1944
in the Western Pacific.
It was a violent typhoon that caught us
near the center of the storm
and buffeted us by extreme seas
and hurricane force winds of 90+ mph.
Three destroyers capsized and went down
with practically all hands, while a cruiser,
five aircraft carriers, and three destroyers
suffered serious damage.
Our ship suffered only minor damage
and no loss of life.
A typhoon at sea is one of the most frightening
experiences a sailor can have.
The wind howls ceaselessly,
and salt spray flies in your face with great force.
It is impossible to keep your feet under you
without holding on to a stanchion or lifeline.
The ship pitches and rolls violently
in the angry waves, many of them reaching
70 feet or more into the air.
The ship climbs up a wave, reaches the top,
and then dives into the trough at express train speed.
The ship's bow goes under several feet of water
and a wall of water races up the main deck
to the wheelhouse under the bridge.
The whole ship shudders under the onslaught.
On the flying bridge, about 50 feet above the water,
the small cockpit, holding the speaking tube
to the bridge allows me, as the officer of the deck,

to communicate with the helmsman
for changes in course heading by voice tube
and by annunciator to the engine room
for changes in speed.
*****

When the storm begins to abate, the ship climbs
to the top of each approaching wave,
and then slams down so violently
that you can actually see the ship bend in the middle.
Fortunately, it did not break in halves!
When your watch is over, you retire to your bunk
and spend the next few hours just hanging on.
If you fall asleep, you're certain to be thrown
out of your bunk onto the steel deck below.
When it's all over, you take a saltwater shower —
the only kind you can get in a combat ship during wartime.
A special soap is needed to get any suds.
Bur, if you're lucky, the water will be warm.
Unless you've tried a saltwater shower,
you can't realize what a difference
a fresh water shower makes.
It was one of the everyday things
I missed most during my months at sea.

The Sailors' Dance

Movement of a ship with a following sea is unique —
particularly one that arrives on the ship's stern quarter.
Long ships with a low draft, like the 328-foot LST,
do a slow roll—like a dance.
Sailors must learn to shift their weight
from side to side and front to back to remain upright.
It's a necessary seagoing skill.

The Piping Plover

Deriving its name from its call tones,
plaintive, bell-like whistles,
plovers are usually heard
before the birds are seen.
Resembling a sandpiper,
the piping plover is a small, stocky,
sand-colored shore bird
with yellow-orange legs,
a black band across its forehead,
and a black ring around the base of its neck.
Skipping along like other plovers,
it moves in short starts and stops.
Blending into the pastel background
of open sandy outer beaches
where it feeds and nests,
the endangered bird breeds
from Newfoundland to North Carolina
and winters primarily on the Atlantic Coast
from North Carolina to Florida.
Counting currently at less than 1800 pairs.
the declining population is attributed to
increased development and recreational use
of beaches since the mid-1940s.
Returning to their breeding grounds
in late March or early April,
the plovers establish their nesting territories
and courtship rituals,
form depressions in the sand close to the dunes,
. and line them with small stones or shell fragments.
Doing a courtship dance includes flight,
looping trough the air.
Peeping when a female approaches,

the male fans out his tail, stands erect, chest out,
and beats the ground with his feet,
as if he's marching.
Following the mating ritual,
the young, usually four in number,
hatch in about 28 days,
and the downy young birds forage
for marine worms, crustaceans, and insects
that they pluck from the sand.
Going undetected by many predators,
due to their very effective camouflage,
the young squat motionless on the sand
while their parents attempt
to attract the attention of intruders,
often by feigning a broken wing.
On Cape Cod, by far the biggest player
in the plover rebuilding effort,
the arrival of the piping plover
has resulted in beach closures
for off-road beach vehicles,
lasting as many as 45 days.
Surviving fledge are flying in about 30 days.
Congregating groups of plovers
gather on undisturbed beaches
prior to their southern migration
and by mid-September
have departed for their wintering locations.
The solution to the environmental problem
is to require the participation and dedication
of many different groups— beach managers,
professional conservationists, volunteers,
and owners of beachfront property—
to guide piping plovers back
to sustainable and healthy population numbers.

The Return of the Herring

For many generations, Cape Codders knew
that it was spring when crocuses and daffodils bloomed,
robbins warbled, and herring runs
were teeming with silvery fish.
One of the two species of Atlantic river herring,
sometimes called alewives,
the 8- to 15-inch herring
arrived early in the spring of 2012,
which started the annual inland spawning migration
weeks ahead of schedule.
During the unusually warm temperatures
of February, and especially late March,
schools of up to 20 fish (not just "scouts") were spotted
heading upstream in Mashpee, North Falmouth,
Bourne, Brewster, Orleans, Eastham, and Wellfleet,
Those are just seven of the more than 150 man-made
Massachusetts coastal herring runs built
to allow the herrings to reach their spawning grounds.
River herring are a vital part of nature's food chain,
the choice food source for striped bass, cod, tuna,
several kinds of trout, and perch —
as well as ospreys, great blue herons, whales, otters,
foxes, raccoons, and may other animals.
Unfortunately, the herring are now in desperate trouble.
Since the 1980s, the population of herring has dropped
by more than 90 percent.
That fact has major economic and ecologic implications —
particularly on Cape Cod eco-tourism activities,
such as birding and whale watching.
What is causing this crisis?
Over-fishing by foreign trawlers in the 1960s and 1970s;
unintentional harvesting of herring

(bycatch or incidental catch) instead of target fish,
such as cod or haddock,
by large commercial midwater trawlers;
physical obstructions, such as dams, turbines,
chemical pollution, pesticides, storm water runoff,
dredging, and septic system outflow,
all harm the herring environment and herring runs.
As a consequence, the species is under final review
for designation by the Federal government
as "threatened" under the Endangered Species Act.
The solution requires several actions:
banning fishing for herring (the law in Massachusetts
except for commercial fishing at sea);
eliminating physical and environmental
impediments and obstructions;
capping the amount of herring caught;
improving monitoring and reporting requirements;
and banning midwater trawling.
We must do whatever is necessary
to preserve the shimmering herring for the enjoyment
of our grandchildren and generations yet to come.

Haiku
Ospreys building nests
Home for a raptor family
Marvelous to see

Fight global warming
Replace, reduce, or adjust
To save energy

Human encroachment
Crowding out other species
Result: ravishment

Whale Watching from Cape Cod

If you haven't yet taken that fascinating trip
be sure to put it high on your bucket list.
It will be one of the highlights
of your Cape Cod summer or autumn
from early May to late October.
Whether aboard a high speed, state-of the art vessel
carrying vacationing tourists in large numbers
or smaller craft chartered for specific hours
and carrying four to a dozen paying customers,
it will be worth the investment of your time and treasure.
These vessels offer qualified naturalists
or experienced skippers to serve as your whale interpreters
by providing expert narrations or answering your questions.
Begin your adventure in Falmouth,
Hyannis, Barnstable Harbor,
or Macmillan's Wharf in Provincetown,
where the big whale watching ships are berthed,
or on the Nantucket Sound or Cape Cod Bay's
smaller harbors of the towns and villages
that line both sides of the Cape.
They include Buzzards Bay, Sagamore,
Sandwich, Hyannis Port, Bass River,
Yarmouth Port, Dennis Port, Harwich Port,
Chatham, Orleans, and Wellfleet,
where the smaller craft are easily located.
Although every voyage is different,
you are almost certain to see
Humpbacks, Finbacks, Minke,
and even the Northern Right Whale,
as they move. broach, play.
and feed along the coast.

Reclaiming the Beach

Autumn is the time of the year
when one can walk the beach
and not see another person
during the stroll.
Of course it depends on the day.
A warm fall day with a soft breeze
will attract large numbers of strollers.
The time of day is also a determining factor.
Midday is likely to be the time
chosen by most people.
But for true beach lovers,
either or both early morning
and late in the afternoon offer
the greatest rewards:
beautiful sunrises and magnificent sunsets.
*****

Greeting the sun outside can fill one
with confidence, promise,
and optimism.
As daylight rises from the sparkling sea,
while gulls and other seabirds fly overhead,
bands of red splash across the horizon.
and the seascape lights up
glowing with a salmon-pink and gold
wash of color.
Almost any Atlantic-side beach,
from Racepoint, Orleans, Chatham,
Dennis, South Yarmouth, Hyannis,
and to beaches farther north,
will provide spectacular seaside sunrise vistas.
*****
Saying farewell to the sun is equally rewarding,

and a Cape Cod sunset is often a magical experience.
You'll never see anything as beautiful
as the blood-red disk slowly slipping into the water,
casting brilliant hues of orange
and purple across the western sky.
Because of the Cape's west-facing beaches,
it is one of the few places on the East Coast
where you can enjoy glorious sunsets over the ocean.
Sunsets in Rock Harbor, off Route 6A in Orleans,
and the outdoor dining area of the Mattacheese Wharf
overlooking Barnstable Harbor (again off Route 6A)
are two of my favorites.
*****

Of course I also like beach-walking in the summer.
But, the fall and winter months are my favorites.
The big crowds, the noisy boats,
and other distractions are gone.
So, for me, and more than a few others,
these are the days when we reclaim our beaches,
the season when we receive special rewards
for sharing our bounty, the Cape Cod beaches,
with thousands of lucky visitors.

Haiku

A wonder to see
An osprey diving for fish
To attract his mate

Canada goose poop
Curse of Cape homeowners' lawns
and golf courses, too

Life and Death

Grace is a first-rate
Relationship with your God.
Cultivate that bond

Identifying My Challenges 2

My genealogy — my heritage includes a history
of coronary heart disease, such as angina,
atrial fibrillation, and heart attack;
circulatory diseases, including, hypertension, artherosclerosis,
and carotid and peripheral artery diseases;
ailments of the eye, including glaucoma
and macular degeneration.
Mental misdiagnoses — faulty early estimates
of my mental capacity —
judged to be incapable of college-level work
by a school superintendent and a junior high school teacher,
resulting in my transfer from the College Preparatory
to the General Course from ninth grade
through high school graduation.
Repudiation of the faulty estimate by extensive testing
at Clark University during my junior year in high school,
which ultimately resulted in recommendations
for college entrance
by my high school principal in my senior year,
when I was selected as one of the three class speakers
at graduation.

Haiku

The greatest journeys
Are never taken alone
There's always a friend

Avoid prolonged stress
Allow yourself to relax
You'll live much longer

Keys to Success

Know who you are
and where you came from.
Listen to your heart.
Discover what you truly love
and what are you capable of doing.

Make a full commitment to your choices.
Do it yourself; don't depend
on financial support from others.
Know what your choices mean to those who love you
as well as to those you love.

Calculate the emotive return on your investment
as well as its financial benefits.
Be sure that your actions will help
and not obstruct or hinder others.
Open yourself to new people and opportunities.

Appreciate your mortality by living
for today and tomorrow instead of yesterday.
Learn how to communicate well
in terms of voice, speech, words, emotions,
facial expressions, posture, and bearing.

Give back for what you have been given.
Learn to commit emotionally and not just verbally.
Enjoy your blessings and your life!
Remember that you only get
one life to make your mark.

My Favorite Menus

Home-style Roast Turkey or Chicken
Cream of celery soup
Garden salad
Whole roaster turkey or chicken
Giblet gravy
Bell's traditional stuffing
Jellied cranberry sauce
Whipped potatoes
Mashed acorn squash
Fresh or frozen green peas
Apple pie with vanilla ice cream

Ranch-style Roast Beef
Beef bouillon
Iceberg lettuce wedges with blue cheese sauce
Tender loin or oven roast of beef
Beef au jus gravy
Baked potato with sour cream
Creamed onions
Frozen or fresh green beans
Chocolate cream pie

Farm-style Oven Pork Roast
Kale soup
Romaine lettuce leaves with artichoke hearts
Boneless pork tenderloin roast
Apple sauce
Candied sweet potato
Apple Raisin Pork gravy
Cubed butternut squash
Creamed broccoli florets

Tapioca pudding topped with whipped cream

Lamb Shanks O'Neill
Corn chowder
Avocado halves topped with black olives
Braised and slow-cooked lamb shanks
Mint jelly
Whipped potatoes
Rosemary/horse radish/raisin gravy
Mashed carrots and turnip
Asparagus stalks
Grape nut pudding topped with whipped cream

Baked Ham Tracey
Cream of broccoli bisque
Garden Salad
Sliced pineapple rounds
Butt half (bone-in) ham roast
Apple raisin gravy
Mashed potatoes
Cubed Hubbard squash
Buttered julienne parsnips
Bread pudding with maple syrup

Cape Cod Baked Haddock or Cod
Clam or fish chowder
Shrimp cocktail with hot sauce
Breaded seasoned fresh-caught fish fillets
Egg and lemon fish sauce
Twice-baked potatoes with cheese
Coined or julienne carrots
Creamed cauliflower or lima beans
Banana cream pie

Perseverance and Diligence

Life for us was not serene and carefree.
We wanted to marry,
but we faced the disapproval
of parents, grandparents,
siblings, other relatives, and friends:
we were "too young, " "just starting college,"
"had neither jobs nor money,"
and "it's wartime."
And worst of all, in the view of her family,
I had no name of my own,
was only recently adopted by my "parents,"
and did not have the proper lineage —
like the one esteemed and owned by her family.
Yet she and I persevered
in our quest for joy and happiness together.
We stayed the course
when the storm clouds blanketed the skies.
We maintained out heading
when other ships wandered off course.
We kept our heads
when the tempest tore our families apart.
Instead of abandoning our pursuit of happiness,
we made each other stronger
and shared and shouldered each other's anguish.
Although we sometimes disagreed, most of the time
we laughed, cried, and cared for and loved each other.
Looking back we recalled intrepid pride,
courage, and perseverance.
We married soon after,
We either convinced them
or they gave up
Anyway we won!

Grandpa Burgoyne's Farm

I did a lot of hard work on Grandpa's
Ellenburg, New York farm.
Although it had neither electricity nor plumbing,
it had fascinating things to see and do,
as well as a whole lot of charm.

The three-room log house was built by hand
by my grandpa with the help of neighbors
in only a few weeks of heavy labor
and set upon a 25-acre lot of land.

Between the house and the barn
was a deep and quaint water well
with a pail and rope affixed to a handle
to draw water for the animals and people
to perform their ablutions and drink their fill.

Threading through the farm was a fresh water stream;
a place for bathing and swimming and fun
after a long day's labor in the sweltering sun.
Surrounded by fields, several for hay,
pastures aplenty for cows and horses,
for milking and plowing, and wagons to dray.

There was also a large family garden for planting
produce and feed as well as vegetables and fruit
for meals and winter supplies for canning.
I milked six cows morning and evening
and gathered eggs the chickens left for us.
but when I approached to collect them,
they always made a big fuss.

A 3-holer out back met the family's needs
when forced to heed nature's call,
and the softest pages
of the Montgomery Ward catalog
were within easy reach on the inside wall.

The kitchen was the special place
where my uncles sat and talked.
In that cosy room was Grandpa's special chair
where he smoked his corncob pipe and rocked.

Grandma loved the kitchen
where cooking chores were shared
with my aunts and female cousins
where breads, oatmeal, meat and potatoes,
even homemade soap, were prepared.

The big table in the kitchen
with the fireplace close by, the meals were laid,
with meat and potatoes and corn from the garden
and the breads and pies that Grandma had made.

The fire in the fireplace kept the ground floor warm
but the two unheated upstairs bedrooms were an adventure
on cold winter nights to anyone who dared there to venture.

I love those special memories
of my visits to Grandpa's farm,
the old homestead where my mother
and her 13 brothers and sisters were born.

The Business of Death

The prospect of death is something that most people
shut their eyes to, turn deaf ears to,
close their minds to, or deliberately ignore.
Yet, they know that it is inevitable
and that one day death has to be faced —
unless it arrives quickly and unexpectedly.
We all learn about deaths of people, famous and ordinary,
familiar or unknown, old and young,
expected and unexpected, timely and untimely
from TV, newspapers, phone calls,
E-mails, letters, and obituaries.
Loss of family and friends is a fact of life.
I lost my mother when she was pregnant
with her sixth child, and I was only 16 months old.
Similarly, my sister, Mary, died in childbirth,
and my daughter, Kathleen,
very nearly suffered the same fate
during the birth of her son, Sean.
Of my Dad's eight children, I am,
in my 90th year, the sole survivor,
one of the two "middle" children.
All of my grandparents, parents, and parents-in-law,
with the exception of two, died relatively young —
in their 50s and 60s and my siblings and siblings-in-law
died young, some in their teens.
I lost all of my close friends,
including my 18-year old brother-in-law,
Tommy, KIA during World War II.
I have personally experienced near-death episodes.
At the age of five,
I broke through the ice on a pond in mid-winter.
When age nine, I swam beyond my capability

in the waters of Narragansett Bay in Rhode Island,
and had to be saved by my foster mother, Josephine.
At age 12, I contracted measles
and very nearly succumbed to the high fever.
During the invasion of the Philippines
during World War II,
I was hit hard in the helmet by shrapnel
from Japanese mortar fire.
Without the helmet, I would have been killed.
When flying over the Rockies in a light aircraft
and flying in a commercial jet
into London's Heathrow Airport
during severe storms,
the aircraft very nearly crashed.
Riding over the treacherous mountains
of South Korea in an open jeep,
driven by a young and careless Army captain,
we nearly went over the edge
of the rough cliff road.
While visiting troops stationed on a remote island
in the Bearing Sea,
and again on the DMZ in Korea,
while on temporary duty with the Army,
and when I traveled at high speed
in the mountains of Turkey in a staff car
driven by a native Turkish driver,
I courted disaster and death.
And when I underwent two risky endarterectomies
at the Massachusetts General Hospital
at the ages of 81 and 89.
I chanced death.
So, we have all observed death
up close and personal,
usually unwelcome but sometimes accepted

as necessary for various reasons.
Unwelcome deaths typically include
spouses, friends, schoolmates, babies,
children, parents, neighbors, relatives,
siblings, and heroes, military or civilian.
It is incumbent upon all of us
to recognize and accept the fact that the people
ahead of us are becoming fewer in number,
and that the people
behind us are becoming more numerous.

Depression

A disease that now strikes one of five people
at some time in their lives.
It's not the ordinary melancholy that people feel
when adversity strikes; it's something
that appears unexpectedly and lasts for what
seems to be an eternity.
People with depression find it difficult to sleep,
lose their interest in friends, their appetites,
even their sexual drive —
and they often become victims of fear and anxiety.
Medication is part of the usual treatment for depressive illness.
Although the theory underlying the treatment —
the correction of "chemical imbalances" —
has been challenged,
antidepressant medications, such as serotonin
and dopamine, continue to be used.
As well as robbing people of the joys of life,
depression may also be responsible for ending lives,
as the recent suicide of 43 year old Junior Seau.
retired NFL Pro Bowl career as a linebacker, may suggest.

Trees

I planted and cultivated a little weeping willow tree.
It was first one that I felt belonged only to me.
Over time it lifted its arms into the sky,
Fingers reaching toward the clouds on high
Like birds let loose from the earth.

The Almighty lives atop the weeping willow tree.
And, at this time of year, spring,
God is everywhere I am now, much older,
Placed here and in other places in the between years
As the end of my life comes ever closer.

But the tree planted so many years ago
When it was only three feet high
Is now 60 feet above the earth
It will still be here long after
I leave this temporary abode forever.

I have planted many trees in my later years.
Enjoying their beauty and splendor
And the real advantages they provide
Monetarily and aesthetically year after year.

In summer their leaves shade my home
Reducing our air conditioning use
In winter their bare limbs let the sunlight through
Cutting my heating costs by real dollars too!

Trees are good for the eyes
Good for the environment
Good for the pocket book and budget
And good for the heart and soul.

A Loving Gift

Living alone on Cape Cod in April 1972
while I was staying during the week
with my ex-son-in-law-in-law in Townsend.
Knowing that men are more likely than women
to suffer a heart attack in their later years,
that my family had a history of heart attacks,
that I had problems with my heart in recent months,
and that we would soon be alone together on Cape.

Deciding to become certified in adult victim
cardiopulmonary resuscitation "Race-for- Life"
system offered by the American Red Cross.
Wanting and needing to be able
to help me if I had a heart attack.
Doing precisely that for me —
an authentic and true act of love

Showing me the certificate the day I retired
and came to the Cape to live full time.
Appreciating the gift from the wonderful
friend, wife, mother, and lover
that God allowed me to have.
She was some kind of woman,
and the rarest of gifts a man can receive.
I have missed her every day
since she left us in October 1997.

All that we now have
emanates from our God's hand
We have to value and share it with others.

Early Images

One of my grade school images
has both visual and olfactory components.
The incident occurred when I was in the second grade
of Saint Mary's School in Milford.
Every morning we were required to go to the blackboard
to do arithmetic sums and subtractions.
One of my classmates, a boy, was sent to the board.
Of course he, like the rest of us,
wore short pants in the early fall and late spring.
As he walked down the aisle and by my desk
on the way to the chalkboard, I detected a foul odor.
Looking at the floor, I saw a trail of "do-do,"
loose stool, leading from his seat few desks behind me
to his backside, now a few desks ahead of me.
The juicy, smelly material continued
to fall out of his pants legs as he walked to the board.
The Sister sent the mortified boy to the "basement"
and called the janitor to clean up the mess.
Of course, we remained in the classroom
with the pungent order surrounding us
and invading our nostrils for the remainder of the day.

Haiku

Purchase some new clothes
You will like the way you look
And your love will too.

Make time for yourself
Enjoy living while you can
You'll live much longer

Trials and Tribulations

My foster father Eddie was unrelenting
in criticizing my abilities
and underlining my bleak prospects.
I was "stupid," "lazy," "worthless,"
and would "never amount to anything."
Without my foster mother, Josephine,
I could not have survived adolescence.
She always encouraged me
following Pop's diatribes.
She was unfailingly loving and supporting.
I realize now that although alcoholism
was primarily responsible for the constant
disparagement and ridicule,
some of it was due to jealously —
of my foster mother's love for me.1

Cataract

In my 90th year, I am well beyond the age of 75,
when 70 percent of the rapidly declining population
has the beginning of cataract.
Cataract is cloudiness in the normally transparent
crystalline lens of the eye.
The condition can cause a decrease in vision
and may lead to blindness.
. Usually progressing slowly, most people don't need
surgical removal of the cataract.
However, when it begins to blur vision,
it's time to act.
I may be closing in on that day of decision.

Punishment

Corporal punishment was a given in parochial school.
A slap in the face for a minor transgression
was not uncommon,
nor were several whacks on the bare knuckles
with the sharp edge of an18-inch ruler.
Other forms of punishment included
a few energetic swats on the legs and backside
with a yardstick or pointer,
and, in the case of one nun, a few healthy whacks
on the palm of the hands with a hatchet handle,
were enough to deter all but the foolhardy
from breaking any rules.
The fact that the punishment was administered
in the front of the room with the class looking on
made the penalties for transgressions even more severe.
Of course detention, an after school session,
was another form of punishment.
And, for the very worst offenders,
there was a trip to the Sister Superior's Office
where corporal punishment, or even expulsion,
might also be imposed.

Haiku

Don't spar with your spouse
Far better to be yielding
Than to be correct

Ten seconds to go
Design your best winning play
Launch a three-pointer

Maxims You (Should) Know

You have a strong voice
Take positions on issues
Boldly and clearly

Do your very best
Even when no one watches
That marks competence

A generous man
Who restores others in need
Will himself be healed

Fear of falling short
Causing procrastination
Is a plan killer

Don't live with regrets
Fix the emotive damage
By self-forgiveness

Understand this truth
You're better than you believe
Enjoy your blessings

A business truism:
People must be monitored
To avoid screwups

The key to long life:
Stay positive in outlook
Don't sweat the small stuff

A Vacant House

Located on the corner of Grove Avenue
and Walnut Street, an upscale Westside neighborhood,
it was a perfect location for a beautiful home,
which in an earlier era it most certainly was.

I walked past that house twice every day
spanning the years 1932 to 1937, during the Great Depression.
At the start, I was 10 and in the fifth grade
and watched the house deteriorate until I was 14.

The lawn surrounding house was a hay field in the summer
and an eyesore the remaining months of each year.
The paint on the siding and trim was peeling,
the front door open, window rails and bars were missing..

Inside, opposite the front entrance. was a staircase
with a beautifully carved newel post.
The hardwood floors were littered with broken glass.
The fireplace with its carved mantel piece
and ceramic tiles attested to its original opulence..

What was once a library contained book shelves
but no books; the kitchen lacked a sink
and the kitchen piping had been stripped for its value.
Upstairs were three empty bedrooms, a master bedroom,
and two smaller ones. probably a nursery and a guest room.

It was disheartening to see what had once been
a lovely house in such clutter and disarray.
I wonder today what has happened to that house.
Was it torn down or was it rehabilitated
and used as a home for a succession of families?

Duke

Duke was my English Pointer
and good friend for 10 years.
White with brownish markings,
he was a big, handsome, smart, and devoted
companion to my wife, six children, and me.
Duke had both good and bad habits.
Positives
Protective of all family members
Friendly to visitors once introduced inside the house
Loveable at night when everyone else was asleep
Obedient to his master, Mom, and Sean
Eating only when fed
Negatives
Chasing and killing skunks,
and after a rinse with tomato juice,
returning to the corpse and rolling on it.
Digging deep holes in the front lawn.
Bringing large stones to the front door.
Chasing and biting garbage men.
Barking at visitors, invited or not.
Defecating on neighbors' property.
Passing malodorous gas in the house.

Haiku

Duke was my good friend
Sixty-five pounds of mischief
Every chance he got

Duke ended his days
At my friend Dave's spacious farm
Loved by the fam'ly

Childhood Mementoes

When I was in the second grade
St Saint Mary's School in Milford,
two experiences stand out in my mind.
I still carry visible evidence of one event.
Returning to school from lunch at home,
I used a shortcut to get into the schoolyard,
which was behind a fieldstone wall
with spike-like stones embedded in its top.
I used a broken drainpipe leaning against the wall
to climb up and into the schoolyard.
One noon, I slipped just as I reached
the top of the wall and grazed my left front
incisor tooth on the sharp point
of one of the embedded stones.
Fortunately, the tooth was not broken off —
but it left an observable surface chip that remains
80+ years after the event.

The other memorable event left only a memory,
which has made me warily avoid repeating it.
A steel fence guarded the sidewalk of the school.
In winter, it was often covered with ice.
Like many other unthinking school kids,
I made the mistake of trying to lick the ice
and having my tongue "welded" to the pipe.
The obvious solution, using warm water
to release the tongue undamaged,
was not accessible.
So, the only option was to pull the tongue away,
leaving skin on the pipe —
and enduring a very sore tongue for days to come.

Irish Folklore

Leprechauns are the most famous
or infamous of all Irish fairies.
They are supposed to know
where treasure is buried,
and they guard this "secret" very well.
It is believed by many older Irish that,
if you catch a Leprechaun,
you must never blink
because he can disappear that quickly.
What many may not know is
that every Leprechaun carries a tiny purse
with two coins in it.
One of the coins is magical —
no matter how often it is spent,
another coin takes its place.
Because humans have discovered this secret:
the Leprechaun, if caught,
usually hands over the other coin,
and, while the human is examining it,
the Leprechaun makes his escape.

Seanchai were Ireland's storytellers —
raconteurs, artists of the spoken word,
who could recreate on call
the magic of the folk world,
including legends, anecdotes, religious,
heroic, and romantic tales.
The colorful, vivid, whimsical, sad,
and humorous fireside stories
of the Irish people are a part
of a heritage unparalleled

in the oral history of the world —
handed down from generation
to generation around the world.
Nowhere has the art of storytelling
been more richly developed than in Ireland.
The world was the stage of the Seanchai
where they could entertain
and charm saint and sinner, poet and poltroon,
dullard and genius, rebel and rogue,
all with color and clarity.
I believe that my O'Neill Dad was one!

Dreams

Everyone dreams every night,
but not all dreams are remembered.
And that is probably a good thing,
because some dreams are threatening, frightening,
disturbing, or otherwise unwelcome.
Strangely enough, some dreams are repetitive.
One of mine involves parking my MGB at work
and then being unable to remember where I parked it.
Another repeat dream has me unable to locate my
room in a large hotel or in a Navy BOQ.
Another frightening dream takes place aboard my LST
in the Pacific War while serving as OOD underway
during zigzag maneuvers to avoid Japanese submarines —
and finding myself out of position in the convoy in the
morning— and receiving a radio transmission
from the convoy commander to report to him for disciplinary
action upon arrival at the next port of call.
Of course there are pleasant dreams too –
which I shall not describe here for obvious reasons.

Irish Courtship

Courtship was "an occasion of sin"
in the eyes of the clergy —
and the older generation.
A boy and girl who walked hand in hand
were risking their souls.
When a young woman confessed
that she was "keeping company"
with a young man,
the priest invariably would ask,
"And what did you do?"

The obsession with sex
translated into an fixation on the purity
or impurity — of women.
When a woman gave birth to a baby,
she was considered to have committed
the sin of Adam and had to be "churched."
So, when the child was baptized,
she was not allowed to carry the child.
into the church.
The godparents carried the child,
and the mother was required
to enter the church through a side door
where, on the side altar,
The priest blessed her
with oil and holy water.
The vestiges of that quaint custom
were followed when my children
were baptized.
As the father of the child,
I was allowed to drive my newborn
and his or her godparents to the church —

with the godmother, not your mother,
carrying the baby.
At least your Mom
(Grandmother or Great Grandmother)
didn't have to go through a side door
— and be "churched!"

Heather, the Server

With a gracious smile, she greeted me.
Green eyes that sparkled, tresses blonde like sunshine.
Skin the color of cream tinted with honey.
I chanced a glance or two,
enthralled by her openness and warmth,
her confident femininity, shining through.
As I basked in her charisma,
smiling in my control and appreciation,
she asked, " May I take your order?"
You may take anything you want, I thought.
"What would you like?"
"The golden broiled scallops sound perfect to me."
"May I suggest our garden salad, a baked potato
with sour cream, and a side of tartar sauce?"
I quickly agreed, impressed with her perspicacity.
After writing my order, she turned away.
I quickly scanned her up and down,
taking pleasure in everything I saw.
"I there anything else you would like?"
"A diet Coke, please." "A Coke. Is that all?"
"What is your name?" I dared to ask.
"It's Heather, and I'll get your Coke."
And anytime soon, you can get me,
boldly and audaciously, I thought to myself.

The Telephone

We had only one telephone in our house in Leominster
— installed on the first floor of a three-decker.
The phone, a 3-party line, was located in the kitchen.
When the receiver was picked up,
the operator asked, "Number please?"
When the phone rang, it rang once, twice, or three times.
Our ring was "one," so we didn't "pick up"
when it rang twice or thrice.
Our phone was a shared phone, but at no cost to the tenants
on the second- or third-floor apartments.
On the rare occasions that they received calls,
we would rap on the water pipes — two raps for the second
floor and three raps for the third floor. If at home, they would
dash down the stairs to answer the call.

Spelling Bees

In grade school we often had spelling bees—
with the boys on one side and the girls o the other—
until the Sister discovered that the boys were "spelled down"
before the bee was half over.
She then divided the teams —
one half girls and the other half boys.
I wasn't a great speller, but I was not one of the worst.
Although I never won a spelling bee,
Eleanor, my secret love,
and the prettiest and smartest girl in my class often did.
I was happy when that happened.
Although she didn't know it, she was "my girl."

A Life Renewed

The life we live is sometimes unfair.
in this an unreliable world,
where it seems that no one cares.
People use you and sometimes abuse you,
ripping your heart and soul apart.
Then they leave you without regrets
and, my friend, sadly, that's that!
But, never, never give up
and believe that life is all over.
Someone needs to lift you up.
Loosen up, let go, and return to her,
the one who truly loves you.
Open your eyes and heart.
She stands with you, the love of your life,
your one and only ever loyal wife.
She has been waiting patiently
and knows the time and place
where she can and will dry your eyes
and put a smile on your face.
She will mend your broken heart
and bring you loving nights
to relieve your suffering
and make everything right.
So, just open your eyes—
you were heartbroken
and must turn yourself around.
She stands with arms wide open for you.
Although you were lost in the world,
you are now unbound, safe and secure,
with love in your heart, now newly found.

Farmers' Markets

Farmers' markets consist of individual vendors
who sell produce, meat products,
fruits, and sometimes prepared foods and beverages.
Farmers markets exist worldwide.
Their size ranges from a few stalls to several city blocks,
and reflects their area's culture and economy.

Almost every town on Cape Cod has its own market,
all of them relatively small in size.
In Yarmouth, it's the Bass River Farm Market,
open every Thursday May through October. 8:30 am-1 pm,
across from the Cultural Center.
It's a great place to buy produce, seafood, baked goods,
prepared foods, flowers and potted plants,
jams and jellies, honey, and other goods,
many of them organic,
all of them fresh and locally produced.

Farmers' markets allow farmers to harvest produce
at the peak of their flavor
and protect their nutritional value and freshness.
Farmers' markets add worth to communities
by selling directly to consumers and minimizing profit loss
by circumventing the middleman.
Consumers can buy direct from the farmer-producer
and enjoy fresh, seasonally grown food
that was produced within drivable distance
from their homes —
and it is more likely to foster good health
and prevent illness than heavily processed foods
available in supermarkets.

Obituaries

An obituary is an announcement,
especially in a newspaper or on the Internet,
of someone's death.
In recent years more and more obits are lengthy,
running more than a full column of newsprint.
They often contain details about family members,
including the names of children, grandchildren, great
grandchildren, siblings, even cousins and deceased relatives.
Conversely, some obits do not make note of
the date of birth or even the age of the deceased.
However, most obituaries contain details
about the accomplishments, honors, awards,
and decorations of the deceased.
Obits often include a photo of the decedent
typically taken when the subject was a young adult.
The photos are often of the decedent in military,
law enforcement, or firefighter uniforms.
Prominently displayed in some obits
are the symbols, insignia, or coats of arms
of social, fraternal, military, or religious clubs,
such as Freemasons, Loyal Order of Moose,
Elks Lodges, Ahepa, Chabad, and Knights of Columbus
— and Military organizations,
such as Disabled American Veterans, The American Legion,
and Veterans of Foreign Wars.
Most obituaries are composed by funeral directors
or family members of the decedent.
Some people write drafts of their obituaries
and leave copies for their
family members and the funeral director —
and update them every year or so.
That was my choice about 25 years ago.

Mother's Ice Cream

My mother, Pauline, was a gourmet cook,
a graduate of the famous Fanny Farmer's
School of Cooking in Boston.
She worked as a cook for a wealthy Brookline family
following her graduation.
According to her sister, my foster mother,
Josephine Tracey, my mother developed the recipe
for a brand of ice cream that was very popular
in Central Massachusetts in the 1920s and 30s.
It was called "Ideal Ice Cream."
The brand was sold at the Little Store
on North Main Street near Saint Leo's Church
in Leominster, so I had many samples of the
popular convection served in nickel ice cream cones.
The recipe was either purloined or "borrowed"
from my mother by the manufacturers
and distributors of the concoction.
My mother never received a penny for it.

Neat Sports Cars

My Dad loved new cars, especially classy cars.
When I was in Saint Mary's School in Milford,
Dad owned two very expensive ones.
The one that I remember best was a fire engine red
Stutz Bearcat, a well-known American sports car
of the pre- and post World War I period.
He showed it to everyone with great pride.
That's how I got my taste for sports cars.
Most of my cars have been Sprites, MGs, and Subarus.
The only other brands I have bought new
were Pontiacs, Fords, and Chevys.

Cursive Writing

Shamefully, hand printed characters are now taught
almost exclusively in public and private schools.
Cursive writing, also known as linking, running writing, or
handwriting, is any style of penmanship in which the symbols
of the language are written in a flowing manner.
Cursive writing is therefore distinctive from the block letter,
print-script, or printing method of writing,
in which the letters of a word are unconnected.
Cursive writing is a disappearing skill, abandoned
by schools and teachers as unnecessary
due to the ubiquity of computers
and other mobile keyboard communication devices.
Cursive writing is a skill as well as an art form
that should be preserved and taught to all children.
And the proper way to hold a pencil, pen, or other writing
instrument, should also be taught.

Young Love

In the third grade, I fell in love with Eleanor Bird.
the smartest and prettiest girl in my class —
and undoubtedly the brightest child
of either sex in the class.
One year, I had the good fortune to be seated behind her.
So, when the Sister wasn't looking,
I would whisper to her in an attempt
to get her to display her beautiful, musical laugh.
Over time, I tried everything to get that effect,
including a few words in French,
which never failed to elicit the desired response.

My Fears

As a child:
Fear of the dark
Fear of Halloween masks
Fear of the dentist
Fear of thunder and lightning
Fear of injections (trypanophobia)
Fear of snakes (ophidiophobia)
Fear of speaking in public

As an adult
Fear of germs (mysophobia)
Fear of spiders (arachnophobia_
Fear of heights (acrophobia)
Fear of falling
Fear of failure
Fear of enclosed spaces (claustrophobia)
Fear of certain breeds of dogs (cynophobia)

Survival

Mending broken bones
Drying tears of strife
Despairing the lack of sleep
Knowing the anguish of fright

I hear the cry in my ears
I see my weeping eyes
I feel the wail in my heart.
Yet I thank God for being alive,

On Aging

Most of my life I have been
blessed with good health —
physically, mentally, and emotionally.
Although I contracted most childhood diseases,
which all too often ended young lives,
I managed to survive measles, chickenpox,
German measles, and whooping cough—
and I was lucky enough to avoid
polio, pneumonia, and scarlet fever.
My first surgery was a 1944 appendectomy
at the Oak Knoll Naval Hospital, Oakland CA,
a week before I departed for the Pacific War.
Fortunately, despite repeated amphibious landings
in the Western Pacific under fire
from Japanese artillery, mortars,
snipers, Kamikazes, and suicide swimmers,
I returned home unwounded.
However, undergoing long-term exposure
to friendly and enemy bombardment
and antiaircraft practice as a gunnery officer,
I suffered hearing loss, which increased with age.
I was also involved in a shipboard accident
that resulted in a lower back injury
that has plagued me continuously ever since —
resulting in frequent orthopedic and chiropractic
visits, x-rays, MRIs, CAT scans,,
and manipulative treatments.
Beginning at about age 65, I began to experience
new symptoms that required the services of
many specialists, including cardiologists,
rectal surgeons, dermatologists, gastroenterologists,
general surgeons, internists, neurologists,

ophthalmologists, oral surgeons, orthopedists,
otolaryngologists, podiatrists, audioloists,
pulmonologists, radiologists, and vascular surgeons.
Surgical interventions included two endarterectomies,
cholecystcotomy, hemorrhoidectomy,
multiple basal cell carcinoma and colon polyp excisions,
a hydrocelectomy, and two pacemaker implant surgeries.
As I complete my 90th year of life,
I appreciate the paucity of nonagenarians.
as well as the blessing of long life,
granted to others and me despite the negatives,

Memorial Day

There was always a parade in the morning,
featuring flags, marching bands, and veterans
of past wars in uniform.
When I was a kid, the old soldiers
included a few veterans of the Civil War,
Spanish American War, and World War I.
But the most time-consuming part of the day
was the annual visit to the cemetery.
For the Tracey family
that was Saint John's cemetery in Lancaster,
where my birth mother, Pauline Eva O'Neill,
and my Tracey step-grandparents,
Mary Killeen and Patrick Tracey, were buried.
Flowers were placed on each grave,
invariably cut flowers from our own garden,
usually lilacs and forsythias.
The most important part of the celebration
was visiting with relatives and friends.
When finances allowed, we had lunch at the Old Timers
Restaurant in Clinton before returning to Leominster.

Irish Saints

Although there are only five
canonized Irish saints,
there are thousands of Irish men and women
who have been sanctified
by tradition and the devotion of centuries.
The canonized Irish saints are St. Patrick,
St. Brendan, the Navigator,
St. Bridgid, and St. Columcille.
Although little is known of St. Patrick's origin
(Devon, Wales, Cumbria, and Scotland
all claim him as a native),
we do know that as a boy,
Pirates seized Patrick
and took him to Ireland
where he served in slavery for seven years.
Against great opposition,
he was finally elected bishop of all Ireland
and, in 30 years, had fulfilled
his mission to establish the Christian church
in Ireland.

St. Brendan, the Navigator,
a 16th century monk, is renowned
as an explorer.
Whether his voyage was indeed
an historical one or a spiritual one,
it has fascinated people
throughout the ages.

St. Bridgid (or St. Bride)
is the most powerful feminine symbol
of the Celtic Church

of the 5th and 6th centuries.
St. Brigid watches over childbirth,
brings prosperity and abundance,
and increases the milk of cows.
Her feast is the spring festival of purification.

St. Columcille (or St. Columba)
was the founder of the Abbey of Iona.
He sailed from Ireland in the 6th century
to bring Christianity to the remote
and hostile lands of the Picts.

Rote Memorization

Committing words and symbols to memory is frequently
denounced as burdensome and unnecessary.
I beg to differ.
There is a distinct and pervasive need
for rote memory in the education and training
of people at all levels from nursery school
to post-graduate and professional-level education.
such as law, accounting, engineering, architecture, medicine,
theology, and other important disciplines.
At the kindergarten and primary levels of elementary education,
children must memorize the alphabet, vocabulary,
and the "times tables" in arithmetic.
In the secondary and higher-level schools,
the rules and laws of language, punctuation, grammar,
mathematics, formulas, physics, geometry, dates in history,
poems, historical documents (e.g., the Preamble to the
Constitution and the Gettysburg Address), legends, patriotic
songs and anthems, the Salute to the Flag,
and in most religions, a large number of prayers.
For such items there is no substitute for rote memory.

The Japanese Tea Ceremony

My first trip to Japan in March 1959 provided one
of the most interesting, colorful, and memorable
cultural experiences of my life.
While visiting Tokyo, I was invited to attend
a traditional Japanese Tea Ceremony
with my traveling companion, LTC Brian Gruver.
We were the only non-Japanese guests
and participants in that event.

*****

The ceremony was held at Somyo Ueki,
3-4-2 Honkomagome Bunkyo-Ku Tokyo
in a beautiful tea house set in the middle
of a lovely small park.
The ceremony, called Chaji, is a tea presentation
accompanied by a meal.
As with every tea ceremony,
the host spends days planning for the event
to insure that the ceremony will be perfect.
Through tea, recognition is given
that every human encounter is a unique occasion,
which will never happen again.
Therefore, every aspect of tea must be appreciated
for what it gives the participants.
Closely associated with the Zen sect of Buddhism,
it is designed to create peace of mind
in both the host or hostess and participants.
The ceremony has played an important role
in the artistic life of the Japanese people
for more than 400 years.
The ceremony takes place in a room
designed only for ceremonial teas.

The preferred number of guest is four.
The guests choose one of their group
as the main guest.
I was honored to be the one chosen.
Proper etiquette requires participants
to admire flower arrangements and the room
but never the gorgeous kimonos
of the tea master or tea mistress.
A light luncheon, called Kaiseki,
is an important part of the tea ceremony.
Exquisitely prepared dishes are served in a fixed order,
and etiquette demands that guests
leave no dish unfinished.
The host or hostess does not eat with the guests,
although he or she enters the room
from time to time to serve the dishes.
*****

Participants sit on their heels on the tatami
with their legs under them
(a very uncomfortable position for Westerners).
The food and the tea are placed on lacquered rays
set before the guests.
The green tea is made over a hibachi in an iron kettle
and is served in beautiful lacquered cups.
It is whipped with a brush
by the tea master or tea mistress
before it is served to the guests
— one at a time.
The server walks slowly toward the guest,
kneels, sits, and then bows —
holding the tea cup with the beautiful part
facing the guest.
When a guest is served, he or she bows,
takes the bowl in the right hand,

places it in the palm of the left hand,
keeping the right hand
against the side of the bowl to steady it
and bows again.
The first bow is to the person who served the tea;
the second bow is a gesture of thanks
to the gods and Buddha for the benefits of tea drinking.
*****

Before drinking, the guest grasps the rim of the bowl
with the right hand and turns it to the left
to avoid the front of the bowl, the most beautiful part.
The tea is then sipped slowly and deliberately.
After drinking the tea, the guest wipes the place
where his or her lips have touched, using the thumb
and index finger of the right hand, and then wipes
them on the piece of paper served with the beanpaste cake.
The guest then turns the bowl back again
so that the front again faces as before,
and carefully appreciates the form and coloring of the bowl.
Finally, the bowl is placed on a tray or low table.
*****

At the conclusion of the tea ceremony,
the fire is restarted to make "thin" tea.
This tea freshens the palate
and symbolically prepares the guests
to leave the spiritual and reenter the physical world.
The guests express their appreciation
for the ceremony and their admiration of
the artistry of the host.
They leave as the host watches from the doorway.

More About Dreams

Dreams can be our explanations of life —
our interpretations of pleasure and pain,
fears, uncertainties, and strife.
While we sleep, they take over our body and soul —
the important things about us that prey on our mind.

Other times they deal with things
that we cannot comprehend or understand —
ideas, thoughts, feelings, and emotions
that are the bits and pieces, the stuff
that is scanned, planned, or banned.

Every dream is different with conflicting meanings.
Yet, all are special melodies that our hearts are singing.
These dreams of ours seem to be far and distant,
but their purposes are important and puissant.
They tell us about our past and present,
things that are history, things that are here and now,
and things that are to come.

Dreams that inform us about the future
are either the most encouraging or tolerable
or the most intimidating, threatening, or terrifying.
Other times, they are positive, hopeful, and encouraging.
So pay close attention to your dreams.
Thankfully, they're about you and not about me.

Haiku

Aggressive game plan
Attack, attack, and attack
Score fast and often

The Wait

As is usual for the last 15 years,
another day begins, and I'm alone,
wrapped in morning silence.
The sun is just beginning to light up
the front lawn and the quiet street outside.
I have showered and shaved, taken my medications,
made my bed, and eaten my cereal.

The morning *Cape Cod Times* now
sits on my lap while I plan my agenda for the day—
the "must dos," the appointments, the dinner menu
and preparation, the household chores —
and the optional items: the phone calls to be made,
the bills to be paid, the correspondence
and the birthday verse
to be written, and the TV sports
and dramas to be viewed.

After reading the news, the editorials,
letters to the editor, the sports, and weather pages,
I become energized by the need
and urgency of the tasks to be performed.
But, before I begin, I contemplate
what I now call "the wait,"
undoubtedly a preoccupation of people
in their eighties and nineties, if not younger.
I emerge from my silent period of reflection
and note that You did not come today, at least not yet.
But You did give me peace and strength enough
to begin this day. Deo gratias!

Now That I'm Really Old

Although I'm now in my nineties,
and that's extraordinarily old,
I still don't wear a hat unless it's very cold.
I don't wear suits either because I have none.
The last one I gave to the Salvation Army
because the pants were too tight for my buns.
I find that I often can't remember lexis,
even the names of people
that I have known for many years.
I complain a lot about "the kids of today"
and the clothes that they wear to please —
especially the pants with the crotch
hanging just above their knees —
and the waistband so low
that you can see the crack of their butts
like the plumber on TV.
I also protest the egotists who represent us,
the politicians of nowadays.
who spend all their time working for reelection
instead of doing what we expect them
to do to earn their perks and compensation.
I can sit around without shaving,
wear slippers instead of shoes,
and drink fruit juice or Coke
instead of martinis whenever I choose.
And when I hear songs on the TV or radio
I say, "That's not real music
like we had in my day."
But the worst thing I do is repeat stories of yore
that everyone has heard several times before.
But that's the custom of all old men, you know.

Ocean Spray

I followed the path that leads past
the scrub pine down by the bayside.
In the tentative mood that morning cast,
autumn wept as summer died.
I paused to hear the wounded cry
of a seagull among the scattered pine needles
long lost among the thorny brush
and the fruit of sea plums awaiting harvest.
Wary now I recalled the loved ones
I had so often seen depart
pressed deeply inside my aching heart.
And as path draws closer to a heart at bay,
my tears mix with the wet ocean spray

My Last Bucket List

1 Stay alive as long as possible
2 Improve my stamina and stability
3 Compensate for my hearing loss.
4 Improve my visual acuity
5 Publish Strands of Memory — My Swan Song
6 Complete and recheck final version of Strands
7 Make a new list of " To Dos" for Maura and Sean
8 Build a key for my computer files
9 Selectively clear my file cabinets
10 Review my "final arrangements"
11 Endure another root canal and crown
12 Give my children keepsakes of their choosing
13 Pay all outstanding bills
14 Say thanks and goodbye

Tracey Family Events 2011

<u>Jan 3.</u> – Brian and Joanne celebrated their 40th Wedding Anniversary.

<u>Feb 12</u> - Sean's daughter Siara and her Papi (Dad) attended the Portsmouth City Father/Daughter Dance for the 4th year in a row.

<u>Mid February</u> - Victor transferred to Seacoast Academy, an Independent Middle School — the school his Dad founded with 3 others a few years ago.

<u>February 18th</u> Kevin and daughters Kolby and Kaylyn left Miami aboard the "Norwegian Pearl" cruise ship headed for Samana, Dominican Republic, St. Thomas, US Virgin Islands, Tortola, British Virgin Islands, and the Bahamas. They snorkeled, went swimming on the most beautiful beach ever, climbed a mountain on horseback, shopped in the villages, and were entertained by top-level ship nightlife performances. and enjoyed fine dinning every morning, noon, and night.

<u>Feb 27-March 7</u> – Sean's family ski vacationed in Vermont (Sugar Bush & Mt Ellen).

<u>March 5- 9</u> Bill Sr. underwent a successful left side endarterectomy (carotid artery surgery) at the Massachusetts General Hospital. That procedure is one of the top five riskiest operations performed— and it was his second such operation (the first was on the right side seven years ago). He feels blessed!

<u>March 18</u> Kathy celebrated her 60th Birthday party in Hollis.

Unfortunately, Bill Sr. was unable to attend. Sean's family party.

June 18 Kathy retired from her teaching position in the Ashburnham/Westminister School District after 33 years of service as a primary grade teacher and mentor to new or in-training persons preparing for the profession or newly hired teachers. She is happy to have the time to travel and also to enjoy some "me" time.

May Maura's daughter, Laine finished school and received her Teaching Certificate. She now holds a BA in Business Administration and is certified to teach grades 7 –12. English.

May 3 - Victor performed in Seacoast Academy's Jazz Band at the Massachusetts Jazz Educators' Competition.

June 10th Kevin jumped out of a perfectly good airplane. Friend Lin was with him. He never thought he would have the "guts" to do it, but it was one of the most exciting things ever.

June 15 - 25 - Lina and kids visited grandparents in Caracas, VZ.

July 3-7 - Victor attended his 3rd Annual Hoop (Basketball) Camp in Maine.

July 21-26 Bill Sr. was admitted to Cape Hospital following ambulance pickup at home after midnight. Else-Marie found him on the bathroom floor. Maura awoke and called 911. Underwent EEG at Hospital ordered by Dr. McCarthy, a neurologist. He diagnosed the problem as some kind of seizure, but not stroke or TIA (transient ischemic attack or ministroke). Because he is on medication for the seizure, he cannot drive for six months. It's a "pain-in-the-you-know-what" because he only has transportation on Else-Marie's days off (Tuesdays and Fridays) unless someone or a family member is visiting.

July 27–Aug 5 Bill Sr. was admitted to Spaulding Rehabilitation Hospital in Sandwich (one of the top rehab hospitals in the world) where he underwent three and one-half hours of intensive physical and vocational therapy daily for 12 days.

July 30 – Sean's daughter Siara wrote an original play, which was performed at the West End Theater Summer Theater Camp.

Aug. - Maura was hired as a PC Specialist by the Rome City School District ending her sort-lived retirement.

Aug 8 Bill Sr. had Lifeline installed to call for help in case of falls or other emergencies.

Aug Sean produced his second movie, Good *Men*, starring Ed Asner and Mark Rydell,

Aug 27-28 Hurricane Irene arrived. Maura and Steve were here and battened everything down, including clearing the deck. Damage was limited to a few branches downed.

Aug 29 Maura moved back to Rome, NY where her new job with the Rome School Department awaited her—as well as a new house, ready for alterations, improvements, and decorations.

Sep 9. Kenny Letellier, Kathy's first husband and father of Tamra and Sean, was buried in the Bourne National Cemetery on Cape Cod with full military honors. Among his awards: Combat Infantry Badge, Purple Heart Medal, Bronze Star Medal (for valor) with three oak leaf clusters for repeat awards. Soldier's Medal (for bravery), Air Medal, Army Commendation Medal, Good Conduct Medal, National Defense Service Medal with 2 overseas bars, U.S. Vietnam Service Medal with 4 bronze stars. and decorations awarded by the Republic of South Vietnam: Vietnam Campaign Medal. Vietnam Gallantry Cross, and Vietnam Civil Action Medal First Class.

Sep 10-14 Bill, Sr. repaired and labeled all of Kenny's military decorations in display cases, researched and printed out the meaning, importance, and requirements for each award for Kenny's children and grandchildren.

Sept 13 Bill Sr. made the first of three visits to Dr. Koff (dermatologist) to have basal cell carcinomas removed from his chest and face. He has had to undergo semiannual checks to have basal cells on his back, hands, and nose removed earlier. Those were courtesy of the two years he spent aboard ship, often in the strong sun of the South Pacific, during World War II.

October 1 - Siara passed her Black Belt Test in TaeKwondo (the 4th in Sean's family to do so).

October 5. Trafford Publications of Bloomington, IL published Bill Sr.'s book, Strands of Memory Reprised, part of a trilogy of poetic anthologies. The first two were titled *Strands of Memory* and *Strands of Memory Revisited*, published by Trafford and iUniverse respectively in 2004 and 2009.

<u>October 25</u>, Kevin formed a new company, Global Luxury Connect, LLC with partner, Lin Li. They developed a business plan and began forming strategic relationships with sellers of luxury items throughout the world.

<u>Oct 29</u> The family gathered for the 14th Anniversary of Kathleen's death. We visited her grave at the Mass Veterans' Cemetery to place flowers, share remembrances, and offer prayers, attended a memorial Mass at St. Pius X Church, and had dinner at the Olympia Seafood Restaurant in South Yarmouth. Because of the bad weather, sickness, or prior business commitments, the only ones able to attend were son Sean, Kathy, Tamra. Maura, Steve, Else-Marie and me — instead of the 15 who had planned to attend.

We little knew that fateful day
That God was going to call your name
In life we loved you dearly,
in death we do the same.
It broke our hearts to lose you,
But you did not go alone;
For part of us went with you,
The day God called you home.
You left us wonderful memories,
Your love is still our guide;
And though we cannot see you,
You are always at our side.
Our family chain is broken,
And nothing seems the same,
But as God calls us one by one,
The chain will link again.

<u>Oct 29-31</u> The October Northeaster hit New England, causing

power outages (thousands of people were without electricity for two days. many still awaited restoration of service, and many thousands were without them for two or more additional days. Bill Sr. lost a large tree in his back yard, which luckily did not take out several sections of his new perimeter stockade fence.

Late Oct thru Dec – Brian sailed his yacht, The Entertainer, from the Bahamas to the East Coast, Nantucket, the Vineyard, Portsmouth, etc.) and then in late October started a voyage to Florida, which was interrupted by repairs in May in the Carolinas, and was finally completed, with brother Bill's help, to its winter destination, Fort Lauderdale.

<u>Nov 20</u> Victor Carrillo Tracey became a teenager and attended the Rite 13 Celebration at St John's Church.

November 25. Sean hosted Thanksgiving Day dinner. Lina, Victor, and Siara at their lovely home in Portsmouth, with the following attendees: Bill Jr., son Tim and daughter Katie; Kevin with daughters Kolby and Kaylyn and Lin; Kathy with husband Dennis, daughter Tamra and her husband Jimmy and granddaughter, Kaila; Maura and Steve, and me.

<u>Dec</u>. Bill Jr. is starting a new venture as a licensed ship captain. He delivered a 50ft sailboat to Florida starting Dec 4th, sailing about 750 miles and then moved Brian's 65ft yacht to Florida. He has two jobs with his brother, Sean, serving as cameraman on two photo projects.

<u>December 21</u> – The Sean Tracey Family traveled to Prague, Czech Republic and Vienna, Austria for Christmas & New Years.
<u>Dec 24</u> 2011 — the best year for Ride-the-Ducks of Seattle.

My Nightly Prayer

Lord, please bless my parents, James and Pauline, my foster parents, Edward and Josephine, my parents-in-law, Thomas and Lillian, my deceased wife, Kathleen, and my friend and companion, Else-Marie.

Bless my deceased brothers and sisters and their spouses — Jim and Terri, Mary and Bob, Pauline and John, Margaret, Frank and Joe, Eileen and Eddie, Frank and Peg, and Jack and Sandy.

Bless my children and their spouses and ex-spouses: Bill, Jr., Suzanne, Linda, and Kathy; Kevin and Lin Li, Susan, Janet, Kim, and Janice; Brian and Joanne; Kathy, Dennis, and Kenny; Maura, Steve, Kevin, and Sam; and Sean and Lina.

Bless my grandchildren and their spouses: Tamra and James, Jackie and Matt, Mikie, Sean and Leah, Laine, LB, Tim, Katie, Victor, Kolby, Kaylyn, and Siara; godchildren Christine, her husband Paulo, and her children Sarah and Carolina; Jackie and her husband, Scott, and my godson, Bill Camiré.

I beseech the Blessed Mother and all the angels, saints. Apostles, Mother of Perpetual Help, Lady of the Miraculous Medal, St. Jude Thaddeus, St, Joseph, St. William, St. Raymond, St. Francis, and my wife Kathleen to intercede with God to grant good health, physical, mental, spiritual, emotional, and financial, to my family, my children and grandchildren, relatives, friends, and me.

I also ask You to bless my friends, Henry and Bernie, Ralph and Pauline, Peggy and Paul, Jack and Jeanne, Ed and Helen Lou, and Phil and Margaret; my cousins Marge and Bob, my secretaries over a 24-year period, Irene, Nina, Myra, Ruth, and Sofia, and their children and grandchildren, and also the people I have hurt in any way over my lifetime (I name those I recall).

Lastly, God I thank you for all the blessings you have bestowed on my family, my relatives, my friends, and me over my lifetime and request that you continue to protect and bless us.

Index

If you can't be good
Always be dependable
And you'll be valued